✧ *Companions for the Journey* ✧

Praying with
Meister Eckhart

✧ *Companions for the Journey* ✧

Praying with
Meister Eckhart

by
Wayne Simsic

Saint Mary's Press
Christian Brothers Publications
Winona, Minnesota

For Sr. Kilian Hufgard, OSU
  If a person humbles herself, God cannot withhold divine
  goodness but must come down and flow into the humble
  soul.

—Meister Eckhart

Genuine recycled paper with 10% post-consumer waste.
Printed with soy-based ink.

The publishing team for this book included Carl Koch, series editor; Rosemary Broughton, development editor; Laurie A. Berg, copy editor; James H. Gurley, production editor; Hollace Storkel, typesetter; Elaine Kohner, illustrator; Gary J. Boisvert, cover designer; Maurine R. Twait, art director; prepress, printing, and binding by the graphics division of Saint Mary's Press.

The acknowledgments continue on page 119.

Printed in the United States of America

Printing: 9 8 7 6 5 4 3 2 1

Year: 2006 05 04 03 02 01 00 99 98

ISBN 0-88489-516-5

✧ Contents ✧

✧ Foreword ✧

Companions for the Journey

Just as food is required for human life, so are companions. Indeed, the word *companions* comes from two Latin words: *com*, meaning "with," and *panis*, meaning "bread." Companions nourish our heart, mind, soul, and body. They are also the people with whom we can celebrate the sharing of bread.

Perhaps the most touching stories in the Bible are about companionship: the Last Supper, the wedding feast at Cana, the sharing of the loaves and the fishes, and Jesus' breaking of bread with the disciples on the road to Emmaus. Each incident of companionship with Jesus revealed more about his mercy, love, wisdom, suffering, and hope. When Jesus went to pray in the Garden of Olives, he craved the companionship of the Apostles. They let him down. But God sent the Spirit to inflame the hearts of the Apostles, and they became faithful companions to Jesus and to one another.

Throughout history, other faithful companions have followed Jesus and the Apostles. These saints and mystics have also taken the journey from conversion, through suffering, to resurrection. Just as they were inspired by the holy people who went before them, so too may you be inspired by these saints and mystics and take them as your companions on your spiritual journey.

The Companions for the Journey series is a response to the spiritual hunger of Christians. This series makes available the rich spiritual teachings of mystics and guides whose wisdom can help us on our pilgrimage. As you complete the last meditation in each volume, it is hoped that you will feel supported,

7

challenged, and affirmed by a soul-companion on your spiritual journey.

The spiritual hunger that has emerged over the last twenty years is a great sign of renewal in Christian life. People fill retreat programs and workshops on topics in spirituality. The demand for spiritual directors exceeds the number available. Interest in the lives and writings of saints and mystics is increasing as people search for models of whole and holy Christian life.

Praying with Meister Eckhart

Praying with Meister Eckhart is more than just a book about Meister Eckhart's spirituality. This book seeks to engage you in praying in the way that Meister Eckhart did about issues and themes that were central to his experience. Each meditation can enlighten your understanding of his spirituality and lead you to reflect on your own experience.

The goal of *Praying with Meister Eckhart* is that you will discover Meister Eckhart's rich spirituality and integrate his spirit and wisdom into your relationship with God, with your brothers and sisters, and with your own heart and mind.

Suggestions for Praying with Meister Eckhart

Meet Meister Eckhart, a fascinating companion for your pilgrimage, by reading the introduction to this book. It provides a brief biography of Meister Eckhart and an outline of the major themes of his spirituality.

Once you meet Meister Eckhart, you will be ready to pray with him and to encounter God, your sisters and brothers, and yourself in new and wonderful ways. To help your prayer, here are some suggestions that have been part of the tradition of Christian spirituality:

Create a sacred space. Jesus said, "'Whenever you pray, go into your room and shut the door and pray to your [God] who is in secret; and your [God] who sees in secret will reward you'" (Matthew 6:6). Solitary prayer is best done in a place where you can have privacy and silence, both of which can be luxuries in the life of busy people. If privacy and silence are not possible, create a quiet, safe place within yourself, perhaps while riding to and from work, while sitting in line at the dentist's office, or while waiting for someone. Do the best you can, knowing that a loving God is present everywhere. Whether the meditations in this book are used for solitary prayer or with a group, try to create a prayerful mood with candles, meditative music, an open Bible, or a crucifix.

Open yourself to the power of prayer. Every human experience has a religious dimension. All of life is suffused with God's presence. So remind yourself that God is present as you begin your period of prayer. Do not worry about distractions. If something keeps intruding during your prayer, spend some time talking with God about it. Be flexible because God's spirit blows where it will.

Prayer can open your mind and widen your vision. Be open to new ways of seeing God, people, and yourself. As you open yourself to the spirit of God, different emotions are evoked, such as sadness from tender memories, or joy from a celebration recalled. Our emotions are messages from God that can tell us much about our spiritual quest. Also, prayer strengthens our will to act. Through prayer, God can touch our will and empower us to live according to what we know is true.

Finally, many of the meditations in this book will call you to employ your memories, your imagination, and the circumstances of your life as subjects for prayer. The great mystics and saints realized that they had to use all their resources to know God better. Indeed, God speaks to us continually and touches us constantly. We must learn to listen and feel with all the means that God has given us.

Come to prayer with an open mind, heart, and will.

Preview each meditation before beginning. After you have placed yourself in God's presence, spend a few moments previewing the readings and especially the reflection activities. Several reflection activities are given in each meditation because different styles of prayer appeal to different personalities or personal needs. Note that each meditation has more reflection activities than can be done during one prayer period. Therefore, select only one or two reflection activities each time you use a meditation. Do not feel compelled to complete all the reflection activities.

Read meditatively. Each meditation offers you a story about Meister Eckhart and a reading from his writings. Take your time reading. If a particular phrase touches you, stay with it. Relish its feelings, meanings, and concerns.

Use the reflections. Following the readings is a short reflection in commentary form, which is meant to give perspective to the readings. Then you are offered several ways of meditating on the readings and the theme of the prayer. You may be familiar with the different methods of meditating, but in case you are not, they are described briefly here:

✦ *Repeated short prayer or mantra:* One means of focusing your prayer is to use a *mantra,* or "prayer word." The mantra may be a single word or a short phrase taken from the readings or from the Scriptures. For example, a short prayer for meditation 2 in this book might simply be "All created things are God's speech." Repeated slowly in harmony with your breathing, the mantra helps you center your heart and mind on one action or attribute of God.

✦ *Lectio divina:* This type of meditation is "divine studying," a concentrated reflection on the word of God or the wisdom of a spiritual writer. Most often in *lectio divina,* you will be invited to read one of the passages several times and then concentrate on one or two sentences, pondering their meaning for you and their effect on you. *Lectio divina* commonly ends with formulation of a resolution.

✦ *Guided meditation:* In this type of meditation, our imagination helps us consider alternative actions and likely consequences. Our imagination helps us experience new ways of seeing God, our neighbors, ourselves, and nature. When Jesus told his followers parables and stories, he engaged their imagination. In this book, you will be invited to follow guided meditations.

One way of doing a guided meditation is to read the scene or story several times, until you know the outline and can recall it when you enter into reflection. Or before your prayer time, you may wish to record the meditation on a tape recorder. If so, remember to allow pauses for reflection between phrases and to speak with a slow, peaceful pace and tone. Then, during prayer, when you have finished the readings and the reflection commentary, you can turn on your recording of the meditation and be led through it. If you find your own voice too distracting, ask a friend to make the tape for you.

✦ *Examen of consciousness:* The reflections often will ask you to examine how God has been speaking to you in your past and present experience—in other words, the reflections will ask you to examine your awareness of God's presence in your life.

✦ *Journal writing:* Writing is a process of discovery. If you write for any length of time, stating honestly what is on your mind and in your heart, you will unearth much about who you are, how you stand with your God, what deep longings reside in your soul, and more. In some reflections, you will be asked to write a dialog with Jesus or someone else. If you have never used writing as a means of meditation, try it. Reserve a special notebook for your journal writing. If desired, you can go back to your entries at a future time for an examen of consciousness.

✦ *Action:* Occasionally, a reflection will suggest singing a favorite hymn, going out for a walk, or undertaking some other physical activity. Actions can be meaningful forms of prayer.

Using the Meditations for Group Prayer

If you wish to use the meditations for community prayer, these suggestions may help:

✦ Read the theme to the group. Call the community into the presence of God, using the short opening prayer. Invite one or two participants to read one or both readings. If you use both readings, observe the pause between them.

+ The reflection commentary may be used as a reading, or it can be deleted, depending on the needs and interests of the group.
+ Select one of the reflection activities for your group. Allow sufficient time for your group to reflect, to recite a centering prayer or mantra, to accomplish a studying prayer (*lectio divina*), or to finish an examen of consciousness. Depending on the group and the amount of available time, you may want to invite the participants to share their reflections, responses, or petitions with the group.
+ Reading the passage from the Scriptures may serve as a summary of the meditation.
+ If a formulated prayer or a psalm is given as a closing, it may be recited by the entire group. Or you may ask participants to offer their own prayers for the closing.

Now you are ready to begin praying with Meister Eckhart, a faithful and caring companion on this stage of your spiritual journey. It is hoped that you will find him to be a true soul-companion.

CARL KOCH
Editor

✧ Preface ✧

It is difficult to offer a brief introduction to Eckhart's spirituality. The organic quality of his thought eludes summary, and his style of expression, which employs paradox and poetic language, soars above ordinary discourse on spirituality and theology. The following meditations should be seen as a foray into a spirituality that is complex and subtle. Hopefully they will not only inspire prayer but awaken the desire for further reading and exploration.

I am deeply grateful to Rosemary Broughton, who assisted the work of this text with her sensitive reading and excellent suggestions; and to Richard Woods, OP, of Loyola University, who generously provided a theological critique on the final draft and whose scholarship on Eckhart offered me invaluable insight. Also, special thanks to my editor, Carl Koch, for his ongoing support and creative guidance.

Meister Eckhart has been an extraordinary spiritual guide for me through the years, one that I was introduced to through the writings of Thomas Merton and the scholarship of Ewert Cousins of Fordham University. My hope is that the reader will also find in him a compassionate and wise companion for the journey.

✧ Introduction ✧

Meister Eckhart:
Compassionate Teacher and Preacher

Describing how Meister Eckhart had captured his imagination, Thomas Merton wrote:

> I like the brevity, the incisiveness of his sermons, his way of piercing straight to the heart of the inner life, the awakened spark, the creative and redeeming Word, God born in us. He is a great man. (*Conjectures of a Guilty Bystander,* pp. 53–54)

Indeed, Meister Eckhart of Hockheim was the most famous and the greatest of the German Dominican spiritual masters. His spiritual message, grounded in the teachings of Dominic and Thomas Aquinas, addresses our spiritual hunger today as effectively as it did seven hundred years ago.

Eckhart was both a mystic and a medieval professor. He was at home teaching in the academic world of 1300, with its concentration on scholastic theology. But it is in preaching that Eckhart gained his fame as a leader in the spiritual life. While held in high esteem as "Master" at the Universities of Cologne and Paris, he achieved notoriety because of his sermons to cloistered nuns and to lay people. His name became linked primarily to a rich vein of mysticism that flourished in fourteenth-century Rhineland and included densely populated portions of countries such as Switzerland, Austria, Germany, France, and the Netherlands.

The extraordinary influence of Eckhart's teaching continued in the centuries after his death. It is manifest in the teaching and writings of his immediate disciples Johannes Tauler, Henry Suso, and Jan van Ruysbroeck. Through the writings of Tauler, the young Martin Luther found inspiration. In the nineteenth and twentieth centuries, the philosophers Schelling, Hegel, and Heidegger admitted that their meditations were influenced by the German master. Others, such as Ignatius of Loyola, Thomas Merton, Matthew Fox, and the Zen scholar D. T. Suzuki, were also attracted to Eckhart.

In spite of his vast intellectual gifts, Meister Eckhart chose not to concentrate primarily on scholarship, research, or teaching. Rather, he favored preaching, directing retreats, and serving as pastor, alongside his roles as prior, provincial, and novice master. He speaks to us today as an inspired, profound, and compassionate teacher of the spiritual life. His zeal to preach the Gospel, his emphasis on prayer, his description of God's simplicity and intimate life with us, and his recommendations for living in troubled times are concerns that parallel contemporary interests and address current spiritual needs with a welcome freshness.

Eckhart's Times

Eckhart lived in a declining culture on the threshold of dramatic change and revolution. Though fourteenth-century Europe was still grounded in feudal structures of power and could boast of magnificent cultural achievements, much unrest, violence, injustice, and insecurity existed. Historian Friedrich Heer writes, "This period of the Middle Ages was volcanic territory, with the threat of eruption always just below the surface: not a year passed, not a day, without outbreaks of war, feud and civil conflict" (*The Medieval World*, p. 28).

Insecurity pervaded the religious hierarchy. The turmoil was brought on by the realization that Christendom, once a unified whole, had suddenly become threatened and attacked by fringe groups, especially among the laity. Official religious power responded with battles against heresies and heretics, the establishment of courts of inquisition, and censorship of thought and belief.

Though the numerous small groups that sprang up were often suspected of heresy, the great majority of these brothers and sisters had no interest in separation from the church. The lack of pastoral care, the fearfulness of clergy, and the threat of condemnation by Rome or Avignon drove many people to a common life of devotion centered on an inward and personal experience of God's presence. These groups offered women, in particular, greater freedom in a pastoral environment that shielded them from a restrictive culture prone to hurling accusations of heresy or summoning them for public persecution. The Rhineland valley was one place where the widespread interest in mysticism flourished and eventually developed into what became known as the Rhineland mystical tradition.

Meister Eckhart was associated with several groups, among them groups of lay women called the Beguines, whose most famous representative was Mechtild von Magdeburg. Beguine spirituality included devotion to the Eucharist, the practice of poverty, and intense religious experience. Scholars have proposed that Beguine poverty strongly influenced the development of Eckhart's unique teaching concerning detachment as a way to God. Through the influence of the Beguines and the lived piety of women in Germany, the idea of poverty expanded from its original religious meaning to include the search for inward, spiritual poverty—this became Eckhart's primary theme.

The Beguines created a new source of literature on mystical experience and were among the first to write in the vernacular. They were also, along with Dominican nuns, a primary audience for Eckhart during the last years of his life, and they probably transcribed many of his sermons by hand. It is easy to imagine that this audience of ardent religious women influenced the Meister's themes and his style of expression.

Eckhart's Life

We know very little about Eckhart's early years. He was born about 1260 in Thuringia in eastern Germany around the time that Thomas Aquinas, the renowned scholastic theologian, was at the height of his academic career. We know nothing about Eckhart's early education.

At the age of sixteen, he entered the Dominican novitiate in Erfurt. The Order of Preachers, founded by Saint Dominic (1170–1221), imitated the life of the Apostles by centering their lives on poverty and on preaching, especially to the rising population of city dwellers. Preaching gave them an enormous influence over their listeners, and Dominic stressed the need for the best theological education for his wandering, poor preachers.

Studying in Paris and Cologne

Because the young Eckhart showed himself to be an intelligent pupil, he was sent to the University of Paris to study the liberal arts after completing his novitiate. He then went to Cologne where, along with studying philosophy and theology, he made the acquaintance of the venerated Dominican academic Albert the Great. As a young man, Eckhart was influenced by a variety of scholarly thought: grammar, logic, natural science, psychology, astronomy, mathematics, metaphysics, and moral philosophy. When his studies at Cologne were completed, he was ordained to the priesthood. The details of the event remain unknown, but it no doubt was an important turning point for a man who would become renowned as a spiritual teacher.

Teaching Theology and Spirituality

Due to his obvious intellectual gifts, Eckhart was called to Paris in 1294 as an assistant professor. He taught while at the same time preparing for the master of theology degree, the ultimate medieval academic achievement. In the interim he was named prior of a Dominican cloister and, around the same time, vicar provincial of the Thuringia province. It may have been at this time in his life that he guided younger members of the community concerning the spiritual life. These talks, which contain the seeds of Eckhart's mature spirituality, were written down and later referred to as *Table Talks*. After serving in these offices, he resumed his studies in Paris and was granted the prestigious title "Master in Theology." From then on he was known as Meister (Master) Eckhart.

Working for Reform

In 1303, Eckhart taught and, as provincial of both the Saxony and Bohemian provinces, worked for reform in various male and female cloisters. In 1310, after achieving success as an administrator, he was sent back to Paris to teach theology and to defend the Dominican and Thomistic teaching against its opponents. Eckhart's Dominican superiors had great trust in his knowledge and wisdom, as is evidenced by the increasing responsibilities given to him. With the death of renowned theologian Duns Scotus in 1308, Eckhart stood without a peer in western Europe in his grasp of philosophical and theological traditions. His influence continued to grow.

Influencing the Times

In 1314, Eckhart was stationed at the order's house of studies in Strasbourg, Germany, and he served as professor, preacher, and spiritual leader of numerous convents in the Rhineland. It was in Strasbourg, a center of Dominican convents and other houses of religious women, including the Beguines, that Eckhart's ministry as preacher and spiritual teacher would blossom. Religious enthusiasm marked by visions and mystical experiences pervaded Dominican convents of the time; this is shown in the works of Mechtild von Magdeburg, Margarete Ebner, and Gertrude the Great.

Eckhart remained in Strasbourg for nine years and taught many students, including perhaps Henry Suso and Johannes Tauler, two of his most famous disciples. Suso's writings, in contrast to those of his master, show little interest in speculation and include an autobiographical slant. Tauler's sermons do not display the poetic expression and imaginative leaps of his master, but concentrate on the path itself, the method by which a soul can be made ready for union with God.

In 1322, the Meister was sent back to Cologne to be regent of the *Studium Generale*, a place where he had studied forty years earlier. This decision was an example of the trust he had garnered within the Dominican order after thirteen fruitful years as an academician, pastor, and administrator.

Summoned to the Court of the Archbishop

Three years after Eckhart's arrival at Cologne, a conflict arose. To his own astonishment and the astonishment of those who knew him, Eckhart, at the age of sixty-six, was summoned before the court of the archbishop of Cologne to respond to charges of heresy.

A list of about one hundred fifty propositions was selected from Eckhart's works by an inquisitional tribunal. At issue were some of his remarks that seemed to imply that humans and God are equal and that a person could become independent of moral law and ecclesiastical authority. In his defense he consistently returned to the argument that he did not intend heresy and therefore was not a heretic. He also made it clear that he was obedient to papal authority and would recant anything judged to be heretical. Despite his plea that he was no revolutionary and his commitment to orthodoxy, the tribunal determined that the elderly friar's comments were heretical.

Explanation and Appeal

Accompanied by his fellow Dominican friars, Eckhart traveled to the papal court in Avignon to appeal his case. The process, including Eckhart's written response, dragged on for over a year. Before the tragic resolution, Meister Eckhart died either in Avignon or on the way back to Cologne. The exact day and place remain unknown.

About a year later, on 27 March 1329, John XXII issued a bull of condemnation. It concluded that some of the statements attributed to Eckhart could be construed as heretical. However, Eckhart was never excommunicated, and the church never banned people from reading his works.

How could Meister Eckhart, a trusted and learned member of the Dominican order and the church, suddenly become a heretic? Though the issue is complex, three factors should be considered. First, a Franciscan archbishop and at least two

Friars Minor were involved in the attack on Eckhart. This fact suggested to many that the debates and tensions (in which Eckhart participated) between the Dominican and Franciscan orders fueled the accusations of heresy. Second, Eckhart was linked to the Brethren of the Free Spirit, a heretical group that influenced the Beguine and Beghard communities. And third, Eckhart's language, though creative and profound, was often not suited to his audience and, as a result, was easily misinterpreted. Even his supporters found it difficult to defend all his statements, and many of his examiners did not attempt to understand his meaning.

The Judgment of Time

Though Eckhart spent time in papal court defending himself, perhaps his most impressive defense was written by his student, colleague, and friend Henry Suso, in the *Little Book of Truth*. Suso provides a clear explanation of the Meister's spiritual teaching and message and a defense of his orthodoxy. At his death Eckhart is said to have appeared to Henry Suso, who asked him what was the best way to obtain eternal happiness. The master replied, summarizing the thrust of his spiritual teaching:

> "To die to self in perfect detachment, to receive everything as from God, and to maintain unruffled patience with all men, however brutal or churlish they may be." (Richard Kieckhefer, *Unquiet Souls*, p. 88)

These ideals provide insight not only into Meister Eckhart's spirituality, but into a spirituality vital to chaotic times.

Eckhart: Writer and Preacher

Meister Eckhart wrote and published many volumes in Latin as well as in German. The Latin works, which are commentaries on the Bible and systematic theology, are the result of his academic activity in Paris. The German works, which are sermons and tractates, came from his pastoral activities. Eckhart's academic works are the basis for his spiritual teaching, and his spiritual teaching is the translation to a popular form of his academic understandings. As a result both types of writing weave together.

Though considered a renowned mystical theologian, Eckhart preferred preaching to writing. His influence as a preacher is indisputable. In Strasbourg and Cologne, where he spent most of his adult years, he was considered the most popular and powerful preacher of his time. His sermons were meant to inspire listeners to transform their life. He told them that if they wanted to understand what he was saying, they needed to live in a certain way.

To this end Eckhart pushed language to the limit, spoke poetically, and used bold paradoxes to catch his audience's attention and to articulate the mysteries of God. Many consider his influence on the German language to be comparable to Dante's influence on Italian. However, Eckhart's profound message and creative style often made his sermons difficult to understand and appreciate. While defending himself during the heresy trials, Eckhart admitted that his language could have been misconstrued by listeners of his day.

Eckhart's Spirituality

For Eckhart the spiritual life is not a set of practices or observances that help us relate our life to God. Rather, it is life itself, a journey back to our Source, our final return to an everlasting home. His spirituality was also grounded in the *apophatic* tradition, holding that God is "not that" and could not be limited to any attribute or definition. As a result God is most adequately reached by "forgetting" and "unknowing," in emptying the mind of concepts, images, and symbols.

Due to the apophaticism that was central to his thinking, the Meister was not interested in presenting to his hearers a series of truths about God to be grasped by the mind, but in finding the appropriate paradoxes through which he could move his hearers beyond the limitations of the mind and simultaneously mark the path toward union with God. As Bernard McGinn explains, "Only when we have come to realize what it is that we cannot realize can we begin to live out of the unknowable divine ground of our being" (Edmund Colledge and Bernard McGinn, trans., *Meister Eckhart: The Essential Sermons, Commentaries, Treatises, and Defense,* p. 31).

There is no complete overview of Eckhart's spirituality provided by the Meister or by his interpreters. An attentive reader will discover that his sermons and treatises represent an organic whole that reveals its richness and complexity in a variety of themes and nuances. Like a symphony, they are appreciated in repetition over time. The following outline describes only some of the primary elements of his teaching:

The Inexpressible Simplicity of God

Eckhart is awestruck by an infinite Being who is able to create the universe out of nothing. He reflects on the path that leads humanity and all creation back to God. What God truly is remains hidden behind all the names we use for God, in a mysterious dark night of unity that Eckhart refers to as a "silent desert" or the "Godhead." Realizing that God is none of what we have experienced in this life, Eckhart contemplates the Oneness of God: "Heart to heart, one in the One, so God loves" (Colledge and McGinn, trans., *Essential Sermons,* p. 230).

Eckhart understands the God of revelation neither as some distant being isolated from creation nor as a God who can be completely identified with the cosmos. Rather, God is the transcendent Creator who is intimately involved in the work of creation, preserving it and guiding it to its fullness. In turn, every creature is absolutely dependent on God's presence.

Transformation into God

This omnipresent, triune God is present and active in the depth of every human soul. "The spark of the soul" is Eckhart's phrase describing the divine-human relationship at its deepest level. The spark of the soul, said Eckhart, is untouched by the physical world and time. It is much like God, who is also pure and simple. The awareness of God's presence in all things and in the depth of one's own soul is the source of authentic spirituality. God is a dynamic being; we, living in time, are searchers, coming from God and going to God.

Relationship with this intimate but powerfully other God comes not through study or religious practice but through detachment, or "letting be." Through detachment we become aware of all creation as finite and absolutely dependent on the Creator. Eckhart's path of detachment, however, does not call for extraordinary control over desires, excessive asceticism, or reliance on good deeds for salvation. It is an ordinary path that avoids extremes. In the end the world is not neglected or hated but loved passionately in the way it should be loved: with appreciation and care, but without manipulation, control, or self-serving. As our attachment to the world gently drops away, we experience greater freedom.

Compulsions or attachments that hinder the self's union with God include some modes of activity. Activity, for Eckhart, does not restrict the inner life if the ego is not bound to it. He held that we should work and yet preserve our inner silence and unity with God. The ideal toward which we should strive is a life of action that flows out of contemplation.

Birth of the Word of God

The constant effort to "put on . . . Christ" (Romans 13:14) and to be like him in our attitudes and thoughts (Philippians 2:5) is at the very center of Meister Eckhart's scripturally based spirituality. This means day-to-day living as a follower of Christ, taking up his cross and following the example of the crucified and resurrected Jesus (Matthew 11:29). It means coming to him and learning about him in the responsibilities of daily life.

Through the effort of putting on Christ, the Christian believer's mind and spirit, thought and life, are gradually purified and opened to the birth of the Word of God in the ground of one's being. Through the Word the way is open to the divine Source and the Spirit. This is what Jesus meant when he said: "Those who love me will keep my word, and my Father will love them, and we will come to them and make our home with them" (John 14:23).

God begets the Word in the Trinity, in creation, and in the inner life of those who thirst for God. These three births, for Eckhart, are one eternal, giving birth. Birthing is not an external activity of divine nature. Giving birth defines who God is. The Word's birth in each of us is eternal because we were created in the image of God.

If we are to experience the mysterious birth of the Son in the "ground" of our being, we must be emptied of everything—even the image of "God." As the soul is emptied, God necessarily pours into it and fills it, "'Blessed are the poor in spirit, for theirs is the kingdom of heaven'" (Matthew 5:3). Therefore, Eckhart declared, we must become the empty vessel that God fills.

Union with God

The soul that is poor in spirit is one that is detached and free. It is one in which both the birth of the Son and the breakthrough to the Godhead take place. Unity with the Son and unity with the Godhead, according to Eckhart, are inseparable; it is not possible to achieve one without the other.

An Ordinary Way

Meister Eckhart addresses the spiritual thirst not only of his own time, the fourteenth century, but of ours as well. His spiritual vision includes an emphasis on detachment and fulfillment that is contrary to an obsession or inordinate concern with possessions and status. He guides his listeners in the exploration of the inner self in an era when institutional structures are either collapsing or recognized as insufficient. He preaches ways of integrating prayer life into an active lifestyle. He highlights an expansive social responsibility that evolves out of a maturing union with God. Eckhart preaches about issues and addresses concerns that are deeply rooted in our contemporary consciousness.

In these and other areas, Eckhart speaks with a wise and fresh voice. Richard Woods summarizes the relevance of Eckhart's spirituality for us today:

In the end, Eckhart's way is the ordinary way—human, unspectacular, healthy because whole, divinely simple, an easy burden, a light yoke. . . . It is the gospel of Jesus interpreted and fulfilled by a man profoundly attuned to his own times and because of that in tune with our times, all times and all seasons. (*Eckhart's Way*, p. 219)

The Overflowing Goodness
of God

Theme: The life of the Godhead flows out and gives expression to the infinite secret hidden within. Going out while remaining within is the key to the spiritual life.

Opening prayer: God of life, give me the grace to understand and participate in this fundamental movement of divine life—pouring out yet remaining inwardly within.

About Eckhart

A mystical poem, *The Grain of Mustard-Seed,* is usually added to the biography of Meister Eckhart, though we have no proof of his authorship. The poem, however, written in a Thuringian dialect, strikingly represents the main themes of his teaching.

The first three stanzas in particular summarize the Meister's doctrine of the "flowing out" through which the three persons of the Trinity are distinguished. Following is the third stanza:

The threefold clasp
we cannot grasp,
the circle's span
no mind can scan:

for here's a mystery fathomless.

. . . .

The wondrous ring
holds everything,
its central point stands motionless.

(M. O'C. Walshe, trans. and ed.,
Meister Eckhart: Sermons and Treatises, vol. 1, p. xxix)

Divine nature, according to Eckhart, has two characteristics: on the one hand, it is manifest and can be known; on the other hand, it remains hidden and unable to be known. Human nature parallels divine nature. Human nature also has an aspect that is manifest and can be known, and another aspect, the ground of one's being, that remains hidden and unknown.

Eckhart refers to the hiddenness of divine nature as the Godhead or divine ground, the One beyond all names and images. The dynamic Godhead "swells up" as the persons of the Trinity, and then, in an overflow of life, goodness, and love, "boils over" into creation. In a further unfolding of this energetic process, the Son becomes incarnate and the birth of the Word takes place in the heart of just and good persons.

The Meister favors the metaphor of birthing to describe the dynamism of the Godhead: "'Life' expresses a type of 'pushing out' by which something swells up in itself and first breaks out totally in itself, each part into each part, before it pours itself forth and 'boils over' on the outside" (Bernard McGinn, ed., *Meister Eckhart: Teacher and Preacher*, p. 46).

This process of divine "flowing out" has two stages. In the first movement, creation flows from the Godhead through the Trinity; in the second movement, creation flows back into the Godhead as persons open their heart to the birth of the Word within. Focusing on the image of birth, Eckhart says that the birth of the Word in us enables a second breakthrough, a returning back to the divine ground, the God beyond God. The spiritual life, for Eckhart, does not consist primarily of activities or practices but of life itself, a journey back to the homeland, to the Source of all life.

Pause: Do the images of flowing and overflowing speak to you of God's life in creation?

Eckhart's Words

All good flows out from the overflowing of the goodness of God. (Colledge and McGinn, trans., *Essential Sermons*, p. 189)

Here is the flowing out and the springing up of the Holy Spirit, from whom alone, as he is God's Spirit and himself Spirit, God the Son is conceived in us. (*Essential Sermons*, p. 227)

It is a marvelous thing that something flows out yet remains within. That a word flows out yet remains within is certainly marvelous. That all creatures flow out yet remain within is a wonder. (McGinn, ed., *Teacher and Preacher*, p. 292)

Go completely out of yourself for God's love, and God comes completely out of himself for love of you. And when these two have gone out, what remains there is a simplified One. In this One the Father brings his Son to birth in the innermost source. Then the Holy Spirit blossoms forth, and then there springs up in God a will that belongs to the soul. (*Essential Sermons*, p. 184)

Reflection

Eckhart was not interested primarily in the abstract God of the philosophers but in the one, living God of the Bible, the God of mystery who was revealed in "I AM WHO I AM" (Exodus 3:14) in the Hebrew Scriptures and who became incarnate within creation in Jesus of Nazareth, according to the Christian Testament. In speaking of "I AM WHO I AM," the Meister celebrates the superabundant energy of God's life with dynamic metaphors like birthing, springtime, a fountain, a horse running free in a meadow, and the blossoming of a flower.

The active Trinity, in particular the second person, Christ, serves as the image or archetype of all things, especially human beings. Because we are from the divine, in the image of Christ, all that is said concerning the emergence of the triune

God out of the Godhead and the mystery of the Incarnation becomes relevant to us.

The life of the Trinity is at the heart of our own spiritual life. Through baptism we receive the mysterious presence of the Trinity—Father, Son, and Holy Spirit. Though we may have become accustomed to thinking of the Trinity as a theological puzzle and may not have seen its relationship with our life, Eckhart invites us to realize that we are already participating in the secret life of the Trinity, whether we are conscious of it or not. We participate by being alive, but much more fully alive through grace. The Trinity may be a mystery, but it reveals itself in us primarily through our hunger for God and for the meaning of life.

As evidenced in several of his sermons, Eckhart is awed by the insight that God's expression in the Son retains the energy of divine nature with no loss. We ourselves in our words find it difficult to express what we feel and know in our heart, and as a result much remains unspoken. God, however, does not suffer from this limitation; all of God's mystery is totally expressed in the Son. This ability to "flow out yet remain within," Eckhart tells us, is the key to all spiritual life. It is the mystery present in the creating and sustaining of all creation. It is the same mystery we witness when we discover the Trinity mirrored in our depths and then reach out to the world with acts of compassion.

To the extent that we discover that we are truly images of God, sharing in the life of the Trinity, we will find that we can give ourselves with greater and greater energy and yet remain inwardly anchored in God. Who does not yearn for a center of peace in the middle of daily life?

✧ Consider the images of God as "flowing out," "boiling over," or "birthing."

✦ Which of these images appeal to you?

✦ In what way do they offer you a new approach to experiencing God's love?

✦ In your journal describe one of the images in a way that makes it personal for you.

✦ Close by writing a prayer to the God who gives you your life and gives life to all in the multiplicity of creation.

✧ Reread the "Eckhart's Words" section slowly.

✦ Repeat the word "home" like a mantra. Do this for several minutes. Let images and feelings rise from within.

✦ Do you feel a deep homesickness? How does the word "home" speak to you?

✦ Write a letter to the God who is your origin and your home.

✦ Close with this prayer by Saint Augustine: "Let us come home at last to you, O Lord, so that we shall not be lost." (Dame Maura Sée, ed., *Daily Readings with St. Augustine*, p. 38)

✧ Eckhart tells us that to go out, yet remain within; to transcend, yet remain immanent; to be in movement, yet be in total repose is the key to the spiritual life. Take time for a walking or sitting meditation:

✦ Bring to mind the events of the previous day and think particularly of the energy you poured out in work and relationships.

✦ Reflect on your ability to remain inwardly at peace while at the same time sharing your life.

✦ Be still in God's presence.

✦ Ask God for the strength and wisdom to remain centered as you move into the day.

✧ Go somewhere where you can regard persons *absorbed* in their work: a library with students, a playground with children in the sandbox, a church with persons meditating. Watch them write, play, or pray, "flow[ing] out [of themselves] yet remain[ing] within." Think of the moments when you are absorbed in something outside yourself, yet very inwardly present. Jot down four activities in which you find yourself absorbed in this way. Pray about a fifth activity in which you would like to become more present.

✧ Draw a symbol or write a poem that describes the persons of the Trinity in the one dynamic life. Move away from thinking, and allow yourself to dwell in the presence of the Trinity at the center of your life.

✧ As an expression of the power of the Trinity in your life, go out of yourself and perform an act of kindness for someone in need. Perhaps you may choose to express yourself in words by writing to someone who is suffering and needs affirmation.

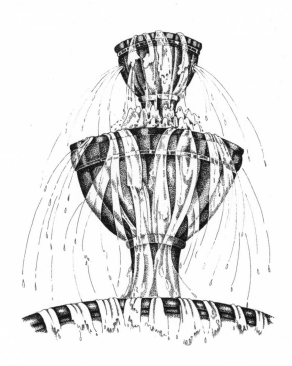

God's Word

For as the rain and the snow come down from heaven,
    and do not return there until they have watered the
        earth,
making it bring forth and sprout,
    giving seed to the sower and bread to the eater,
so shall my word be that goes out from my mouth;
    it shall not return to me empty,
but it shall accomplish that which I purpose,
    and succeed in the thing for which I sent it.

(Isaiah 55:10–11)

"Everyone who drinks of this water will be thirsty again, but those that drink of the water that I will give them will never be thirsty. The water that I will give will become in them a spring of water gushing up to eternal life." (John 4:13–14)

Closing prayer: Teach me, Spirit of God, the paradoxical art of reaching out while remaining within. With your guidance let me deepen my sense of self and discover your reality in the reality of my own being.

✧ **Meditation 2** ✧

Creation in and for Christ

Theme: God speaks in two ways: internally and silently within the Trinity, externally and aloud in the creation of the universe. God, through the same Word spoken eternally, brings the universe into being in time.

Opening prayer: Creator, let me never lose touch with the Word that unites me with myself, with others, with all creation, and with you.

About Eckhart

Though Eckhart encouraged a contemplative state in which words and concepts can, at best, only hint at what God is, he did not imagine that God remained distant from us and creation. God is infinitely distant but, at the same time, immediately present. Creation itself is a constant revelation of the divine.

When creatures are seen properly, as contingent beings dependent on God, they radiate the divine they possess within. They are poetry. Just as a word becomes poetry when it bears a depth of meaning, so aspects of creation are poetry when they are recognized as hiding a treasure within themselves while at the same time revealing it. When Eckhart used metaphors in his sermons, such as a blossoming plant, a horse frolicking in a field, and a singular stone, they revealed not only his wordplay but his vision of the world as poetry, as the language of God.

Like many of his contemporaries, Eckhart assumed that, along with the Scriptures, Creation was a book of God, and that with a proper reading, it would reveal the divine. Moreover, he believed that those who read the book of Creation in depth touch the Word, which is its ultimate meaning. In one of his sermons, Eckhart said that those who were familiar with Creation would not need a sermon because they were already experiencing the fullness of God in the book of Creation.

Pause: What signs do you see of God's presence in the world as you look around in this environment and this season?

Eckhart's Words

The Father speaks the Son out of all his power, and he speaks in him all things. All created things are God's speech. The being of a stone speaks and manifests the same as does my mouth about God. (Colledge and McGinn, trans., *Essential Sermons*, p. 205)

God has only ever spoken one thing. His speech is only one. In this one speaking he speaks his Son and, together with him, the Holy Spirit and all creatures; and there is only one speaking in God. (McGinn, ed., *Teacher and Preacher*, p. 293)

Whoever knew but one creature would not need to ponder any sermon, for every creature is full of God and is a book. (*Teacher and Preacher*, p. 259)

Reflection

For Eckhart, the Son, the Word, is the central mystery. Bernard McGinn writes, "What is distinctive of the Meister's own teaching on creation, however, is the way in which his analysis . . . highlights the exemplary activity of the divine Word or Logos"

(Colledge and McGinn, trans., *Essential Sermons,* p. 39). Through the Word the Godhead is expressed and lives eternally as the Trinity; through the same person, the universe is expressed and becomes creation.

The Word, then, is at the origin of the universe, and is the one who holds all else together. It is the creative power of God that draws all things back to the Father: "The Father speaks the Son always, in unity, and pours out in him all created things. . . . All their life and their being is a calling and a hastening back to him from whom they have issued" (*Essential Sermons,* p. 205).

The judges who reviewed Eckhart's work for heretical implications assumed that Eckhart believed that the universe emerged from God in the same way the Son did. This would amount to a pantheistic interpretation, confusing God with the universe. However, scholars today recognize that Eckhart, in contrast to pantheism—the belief that everything is God—developed the Christian teaching known as panentheism, "the belief that God is present in all things, and conversely that all things mediate God's presence to those able and willing to grasp the reality of that presence" (Woods, *Eckhart's Way,* p. 52).

Only through the Word, then, can we find a path of unity with ourselves, others, all creation, and God. When we lose touch with this reality, our life quickly loses its center and falls into anxiety, chaos, and fear. If we began to open our life to the Word and discovered a dim reflection of the divine light at the center of our being, what perspective would we then have on the world? To know creation in itself, says Eckhart, is "evening knowledge"; to know creation in God is "morning knowledge" (*Essential Sermons,* p. 245).

To know creation in God, for Eckhart, involves a twofold vision. First, the world appears fleeting and fragile, completely dependent on the loving presence of the Creator. Created things seem empty because they receive their being and perfection only in God. Eckhart goes so far as to call created things nothing: "All creatures are pure nothing. I do not say they are a trifle or they are anything: they are pure nothing. What has no being, is not. All creatures have no being, for their being consists in the presence of God" (Walshe, trans. and ed., *Sermons and Treatises,* vol. 1, p. 284).

Eckhart is not dismissing the beauty and glory of creation. On the contrary, he is concerned that it is seen from the right vantage point: creatures cannot exist independent of God's being. They are mirror images or reflections of the divinity, he tell us, and therefore completely dependent on God's presence.

Second, to know creation in God opens our eyes to the beauty around us. In Eckhart's perception the world flashes with divine light, "The man who has God essentially present to him grasps God divinely, and to him God shines in all things; for everything tastes to him of God" (*Essential Sermons*, p. 253). Even a stone or the smallest particle of matter speaks of the Creator. Creatures are creative words or adverbs because they want to be near the Word. This vision of the beauty of the world so inspires Eckhart that he exclaims, "Seize God in all things" (adapted from McGinn, ed., *Teacher and Preacher*, p. 293). Tune in to the creative rhythm of the universe, he exclaims, and join in the dance.

Because God, vibrant with life, constantly pours into the cosmos and into our own soul—"God so created the world that he still without ceasing creates it" (*Essential Sermons*, p. 229)—should we not be participating in this divine work by extending ourselves in love toward creation? Eckhart's message to us, living in a time when the predominate relationship with creation is one of control and use, is to remember that we share divine life with the rest of creation and are constantly kept in existence by this love. With this in mind, it is hard to lord ourselves over creatures; instead we should humbly recognize their dignity and extend our love to them.

✧ Find time for an outside activity that you have been postponing: a walk in the forest, a visit to the beach, a picnic, a long look at the night sky. Give yourself the opportunity to "seize God in all things," or, in the words of Teilhard de Chardin: "Let us leave the surface and . . . plunge into God" (*Hymn of the Universe*, p. 139).

✧ Reread the "Eckhart's Words" section, then pray the following prayer of Teilhard de Chardin:

Lord Jesus, when it was given me to see where the dazzling trail of particular beauties and partial harmonies was leading, I recognized that it was all coming to centre on a single point, a single person: yourself. Every presence makes me feel that you are near me; every touch is the touch of your hand. (*Hymn of the Universe*, p. 153)

✦ Continue in the spirit of Teilhard by writing a reflection on your own experience of the divine in the natural world.

✦ Close with the following poem by the seventeenth-century mystical poet Angelus Silesius, who echoes the Meister's spirit:

In God all that is, is God.
In [God] the smallest creature
of earth and sea
is worth no atom less
than you or me.

(Frederick Franck, trans.,
The Book of Angelus Silesius, p. 72)

✧ All creation speaks of God. Think of the world as a poem. Which favorite "words" would you include in your personal song to God? List these words, and conclude with praise and thanksgiving to the Creator.

✧ Dance, paint, sing, write in response to the dance of creation.

✧ Think of the divine life you share with creation. How do you extend respect and reverence toward the earth? Do you garden, conserve energy, recycle, support organizations with an ecological vision?

God's Word

In the beginning when God created the heavens and the earth, the earth was a formless void and darkness covered the face of the deep, while a wind from God swept over the face of the waters. Then God said, "Let there be light"; and there was light. (Genesis 1:1–3)

In the beginning was the Word, and the Word was with God, and the Word was God. He was in the beginning with God. All things came into being through him, and without him not one thing came into being. What has come into being in him was life, and the life was the light of all people. (John 1:1–4)

Closing prayer: Through my relationship with you, Christ the Word, may I discover the divinity of creation and learn to appreciate and respect creatures in imitation of your abundant love for all beings.

✧ Meditation 3 ✧

Turning Inward

Theme: At the deepest and most intimate level, we are in touch with God, but because of the nature of the Fall within Creation as recorded in the Scriptures, we are mostly inattentive to this relationship. It is necessary, then, to take the spiritual journey and rediscover our intimacy with the infinite.

Opening prayer: "I sought for you abroad, but you were within me though I was far from you. Then you touched me, and I longed for your peace, and now all my hope is only in your great mercy." (Sée, ed., *St. Augustine*, p. 21)

About Eckhart

During this time of spiritual famine, an atmosphere of worldliness pervaded monasteries and influenced the life of religious. Towns suffered from the lack of pastoral care and—as in the case of Strasbourg, Eckhart's hometown—were subject to a papal interdict that forbade celebrating Mass and administering the other sacraments. At this time small groups sprang up searching for peace of soul and an inward experience of God.

While castles and churches were crumbling, Eckhart's preaching concentrated on the inmost citadel of the soul, which was unshakable and impregnable. This inner kingdom, where the flame of the Godhead burns, linked the heart to God in joy and freedom. The following excerpt is taken from one of the legends that surrounds Eckhart's life, entitled "Good Morning:"

"A king must have a kingdom. What is your realm, brother?"

"In my soul."

He said, "In what way, brother?"

"When I have closed the doors of my five senses and desire God with all my heart, I find God in my soul, as radiant and joyous as He is eternal life."

He said, "You must be a saint. Who made you one, brother?"

"Sitting still and raising my thoughts aloft and uniting with God—that has drawn me up to heaven, for I could find no rest in anything that was less than God. Now I have found Him I have rest and joy in Him eternally, and that surpasses all temporal kingdoms.

(Walshe, trans. and ed., *Sermons and Treatises*, vol. 3, pp. 137–138)

Pause: Consider the restlessness of your heart and your attachment to things that can never bring you peace. Recall your need to have God at home in the depths of your heart.

Eckhart's Words

A person who is not at home with inward things does not know what God is. It is just like a man who has wine in his cellar and, having neither drunk nor even tried it, does not know that it is good. This is exactly the situation of people who live in ignorance: They do not know what God is and they think and fancy they are [really] living. Such knowledge is not from God. One must have a pure and translucent knowledge of divine truth. (McGinn, ed., *Teacher and Preacher*, p. 262)

"God is closer to me than I am to myself: my being depends on God's being near me and present to me. So he is also in a stone or a log of wood, only they do not know it.

If the wood knew God and realized how close He is to it as the highest angel does, it would be as blessed as the highest angel. And so man is more blessed than a stone or a piece of wood because he is aware of God and knows how close God is to him. And I am the more blessed, the more I realize this, and I am the less blessed, the less I know this. I am not blessed because God is in me and is near me and because I possess Him, but because I am aware of how close He is to me, and that I *know* God." (Woods, *Eckhart's Way*, p. 62)

God's seed is in us. If it were tended by a good, wise and industrious laborer, it would then flourish all the better, and would grow up to God, whose seed it is, and its fruits would be like God's own nature. The seed of the pear tree grows into a pear tree, the seed of a nut tree grows to be a nut tree, the seed of God grows to be God. But if it happens that the good seed has a foolish and evil laborer, then weeds grow up and overgrow and smother the good seed, so that it cannot grow up to the light and to its full size. Yet Origen, a great teacher, says: "Because God himself has sowed and planted and given life to this seed, even though it may be overgrown and hidden, it will never be destroyed or extinguished completely; it will glow and shine, gleam and burn, and it will never cease to turn toward God." (Colledge and McGinn, trans., *Essential Sermons*, p. 241)

Reflection

Just as all creation exists in, with, and through God, so humans, too, retain an inner unity with God at the deepest level. Even the awareness of our own sinfulness should not delude us into thinking that we exist far away from God.

Eckhart refers to the fundamental reality of our existence in God as the "ground" or "spark." Just as there is a dark and unknowable ground in the Godhead, so too in the soul is a hidden and unnameable spark that is the source for the powers of understanding, memory, and will. For the Meister, God and the person are united on the deepest level "where God's ground and the soul's ground are one" (Colledge and McGinn, trans., *Essential Sermons,* p. 192). Eckhart, however, was not abolishing all distinctions between God and the person, as the inquisitors suggested.

Eckhart speaks of knowing God's nearness. The Hebrew prophets also urged us to know God. This approach may sound impossible. After all, can we really know the infinite? The problem is our limited idea of what it means to know. When we talk about knowledge today, it usually means factual knowledge related to practical skills or the ability to theorize and speculate on the world around us.

Yet, a higher kind of knowing, a contemplative knowing that includes faith and love and is beyond sensate knowledge and rational ideas, allows us to "touch" God. When other forms of knowledge—sense impressions, images, and ideas—are put aside, says Eckhart, the loving knowledge of God can shine forth: "I accept God into me in knowing; I go into God in loving" (*Essential Sermons,* p. 188). Such knowledge is not knowledge about an object that exists apart from us but a laserlike, intuitive gaze, a true mystical intuition that unites the soul to God.

Though we usually know ourselves through what we see, taste, touch, and smell; through the ideas and images that flow through our mind, through the emotions we feel and express to one another, an aspect of ourselves exists that we do not know. It reaches beyond self-consciousness into some hidden dimension of the human identity. It is the origin of all other forms of knowledge. Even if we try to identify this sense of self, words elude us and we stand in wonder. We can call it a "power of the soul" as Eckhart does, or we can simply acknowledge it as a sense of being present to ourselves or to an infinite horizon within. Eckhart's spiritual vision invites each of us to travel to this distant horizon and to experience firsthand the freedom of the mystery of God within.

Each of us longs to live out of a center. Those who begin to take spiritual growth seriously, however, soon recognize that remaining in touch with the divine Presence at the ground of our being involves detaching ourselves from the numerous things that distract our spiritual vision. Eckhart understands union with God as our conformity to the will of God. We become united to God to the extent that our intentions and actions reflect what we believe God is asking from us. We become one with God, explains Eckhart, in the same way that fire transforms wood: "The wood does not change the fire into itself, but the fire changes the wood into itself. So are we changed into God, that we shall know him as he is" (*Essential Sermons*, p. 189).

Encountering God in this way involves more than an occasional retreat or daily prayer; it entails a wakefulness, a heightening of our attention each moment of the day so that we are aware of God everywhere. Using the metaphor of a seed planted to refer to the image of God within, Eckhart concentrates on the discipline and work necessary for spiritual growth. If the seed of God is not tended properly, it will be engulfed by weeds such as anxiety, fear, and personal ambition, and eventually it will be smothered. However, we should never lose hope, the Meister counsels, because, due to its divine nature, the seed will survive no matter how much it is neglected.

✧ Close your eyes . . . take time to relax . . . then read the following text slowly:

Imagine that your desire for God is a seed planted in the dark soil. . . . There is no seeing in this darkness, and you feel as if your life is somehow incomplete, even restricted. . . .

Yet this desire, which may have lain dormant for a long time, pushes outward with questions and a strong need. As it pushes it finds unexpected nurturing from its surroundings and feeds on it. . . .

As it pushes it puts out roots to take advantage of all the nourishment it can. . . . Sometimes the roots find good soil, . . . sometimes their progress is hindered by rocks or by other roots.

Gradually the roots find strength in the dark earth, and a small green stalk reaches the rim of the soil and pokes its head through the grains of earth. . . . Finally it sees the first evidence of light and air. Here it is at the edge of a new world, a frontier that beckons toward a greater reality. . . . The questions and fears are overwhelming. . . . Is this reality good for me? Will I survive in this new world?

A decision must be made: Grow into this wondrous light or return to the security of the dark, former existence. . . . What choice have I made? How have I incorporated my choice into daily life?

✧ Read the first quote in the "Eckhart's Words" section and relate it to your own desire for God.

✦ Ponder this prayer by Saint Augustine in light of your own forgetfulness, "I call upon you, O God, my mercy, you who created me, and did not forget me when I forgot you" (Sée, ed., *St. Augustine*, p. 57).

✦ Pray that you will be awake to the weeds—thoughts and actions that hinder your growth—and will possess the wisdom and humility to call on God's help.

✧ Think about the ways that God has shown you love throughout your life. Compare your awareness of God's love for you in the present with your awareness of it in the past— when you were a child, a teenager, a young adult. Thank God for your deepening knowledge of divine intimacy.

✧ Write a letter to the God who has pursued you throughout your life. Talk about the difficult times of your life when you needed to know for certain that God was truly present.

✧ Pray for those who have nourished the roots of your life and reinforced your journey inward. Bring the image of each person to mind, and say a short prayer of thanksgiving.

God's Word

"Now the parable is this: The seed is the word of God. The ones on the path are those who have heard; then the devil comes and takes away the word from their hearts, so that they may not believe and be saved. The ones on the rock are those who, when they hear the word, receive it with joy. But these have no root; they believe only for a while and in a time of testing fall away. As for what fell among the thorns, these are the ones who hear; but as they go on their way, they are choked by the cares and riches and pleasures of life, and their fruit does not mature. But as for that in the good soil, these are the ones who, when they hear the word, hold it fast in an honest and good heart, and bear fruit with patient endurance." (Luke 8:11–15)

Do not lie to one another, seeing that you have stripped off the old self with its practices and have clothed yourselves with the new self, which is being renewed in knowledge according to the image of its creator. (Colossians 3:9–10)

Closing prayer: Gracious and loving God, give me the grace to know myself in you and the strength to nurture the seed of a new life in Christ. Let me remain awake to the infinite horizon that lies within, and lead me into your silent, luminous presence.

Imitating Christ

Theme: Because he emphasizes the christological dimension of all reality, Eckhart teaches that we should be like Christ in our attitudes and our thoughts.

Opening prayer: My heart yearns for you, Christ Jesus. Teach me to grow in your likeness and to live in imitation of you.

About Eckhart

In the later Middle Ages, imitation of Christ meant primarily an identification with Christ's passion. Christ submitted himself to the will of the Father even in the face of extreme adversity, and anyone who would follow Christ should be willing to do the same. Thus, in that era, imitation involved submitting to whatever suffering or adversity that came with doing God's will.

Authors spoke of the humanity of Jesus, particularly his suffering humanity, as the door that gave access to his divinity. Suffering was viewed as the means of sanctification. Union with God came not from good works or prayer but from suffering. Suffering was the primary way to demonstrate love because it was somehow pleasing to God. It was the path of

Christ, and it should be the path of all who would follow him. This spirituality may be difficult for us to understand today, but in the context of fourteenth-century piety, it represented a serious response to understanding the will of God in one's life and to Christian belief.

Meditations on the suffering of the crucified Savior became popular. These meditations could take place communally in a liturgical setting or could be done privately, thus pervading a person's life and thinking. A good example can be found in *The Exemplar* of Henry Suso. Suso, a disciple of Eckhart, writes a dialog in which Eternal Wisdom responds to the questions of a servant, "No one can reach the heights of the divinity or unusual sweetness without first being drawn through the bitterness I experienced as man" (p. 214). Later the meditation becomes more vivid as the reader is drawn into the reality of Christ's suffering: "My right foot was gored through and my left foot savagely pierced. I hung there powerless, my divine legs exhausted" (Frank Tobin, trans. and ed., *Henry Suso: The Exemplar*, p. 218).

Along with meditation, visions of the Passion played an important role in the lives of saints. When Catherine of Siena prayed that she might share in Christ's sufferings, she received a vision in which Christ appeared to her, told her to stretch out her hand, and pressed a nail into her palm. Though the wound was invisible to others, it caused her great pain.

Eckhart appreciated reflection on the life of Christ for beginners and stressed that one's life should conform to Christ, but contrary to the tendency of his times, he did not linger on the pain and suffering. He concentrated instead on an intuitive awareness of Christ at the ground of one's being. He played down the importance of visions and ecstasy and concentrated instead on finding Christ at the heart of the daily routine of life.

Pause: Ask yourself, How have I followed Christ's example in my life up to now?

Eckhart's Words

If a master craftsman makes figures out of wood or stone, he does not introduce the figure into the wood, but he cuts away the fragments that had hidden and concealed the figure; he gives nothing to the wood, rather he takes away from it, cutting away its surface and removing its rough covering, and then what had lain hidden beneath shines out. (Colledge and McGinn, trans., *Essential Sermons*, p. 243)

One ought indeed to imitate our Lord, but still not in everything he did. Our Lord, we are told, fasted for forty days. But no one ought to undertake to imitate this. Many of his works Christ performed with the intention that we should imitate him spiritually, not physically. And so we ought to do our best to be able to imitate him with our reason, for he values our love more than our works. Each of us ought in our own ways to imitate him. (*Essential Sermons*, pp. 267–268)

It is part of our being a son for us to suffer. Because God's Son could not suffer in his divinity and in eternity, the heavenly Father therefore sent him into time, to become man and to be able to suffer. So if you want to be son of God and you do not want to suffer, you are all wrong. (*Essential Sermons*, p. 231)

Reflection

For Eckhart, the Incarnation of the Son is the fundamental mystery. All else flows from God coming into the world. The birth of Jesus Christ marks God's union with humanity. Why is the mystery of the Incarnation central? Eckhart is interested primarily in union with God. This happens first in the event of the birth of Jesus Christ as recorded in the Scriptures, and second, in the birth of the Word in the human soul, which takes place at baptism. The Incarnation in Jesus and the birth of the Word in us here and now are two aspects of one mystery. We participate in this mystery by growing in likeness to God's Word become incarnate in Jesus Christ.

Concretely, this participation entails, as Saint Paul says, "putting on Christ," or in Eckhart's words, "By putting self aside, a person puts inside himself Christ, God, happiness, and holiness" (McGinn, ed., *Teacher and Preacher*, p. 284). He adds that this may be the promise, but that we find it difficult to believe—it is too amazing!

Along with mystics and saints before him, Eckhart counsels that we need to take up the cross daily and follow the example of the crucified and resurrected Lord, "God died so that I might die to the whole world and to all created things" (*Teacher and Preacher*, p. 289). Though Eckhart does not focus on the physical details of Christ's suffering and death, as was common practice in his day, he does not neglect its importance. He stresses that anyone who is serious about following Christ needs to take up the cross.

To illustrate the imitation of Christ, the becoming like Christ, Eckhart gives an example: It is like an artist who begins work on a block of marble attempting to release a form that the artist envisions within it. The artist cuts away pieces of stone until the inner form is fully realized. The inner form of a human being is the image of Christ.

By removing the obstacles that keep us from "putting on Christ," the Christian believer's mind and spirit, thought and life are gradually purified and opened to the birth of the Word in the ground of one's being. This is at the heart of Eckhart's teaching. The eternal Word is not only the image of the Father but also the archetype, the pattern, of each human person. We may believe that the Word assumed human nature in Jesus, but do we also believe that he grounds the most secret, inward part of our human selves? Thomas Merton once wrote that he, like Eckhart, was interested in "Christ not as object of seeing or study, but Christ as center in whom and by whom one is illuminated" (William H. Shannon, ed., *The Hidden Ground of Love*, p. 643). Through the Word the way is open to the Father and the Spirit: "'Those who love me will keep my word, and my Father will love them, and we will come to them and make our home with them'" (John 14:23).

Because Jesus Christ is not only our destiny but also our way to fulfill it, Eckhart espoused an ordinary path open to men and women everywhere and at any time. Eckhart had little interest in special experiences such as visions and ecstasy. He concentrated instead on the loving Presence that is communicated in the ordinary events of daily life, as well as in the church and the sacraments. As a priest the Meister had a deep reverence for the sacraments, especially the Eucharist. In one of his sermons, he stated that a person who receives the Eucharist with the proper intention will necessarily receive extraordinary and abundant graces, and the more frequently a person receives, the better. Concerning the reception of the Eucharist, he advised, "You should not attach such importance to what you feel; rather, consider important what you love and what you intend" (Colledge and McGinn, trans., *Essential Sermons*, p. 270). Spirituality, even mystical union, was not limited to a few religious individuals but was open to all who took the ordinary way seriously.

✧ Relax, settle into your deepest center, and repeat the following phrase either aloud or in your heart: "'Come to me, all you that are weary and are carrying heavy burdens, and I will give you rest'" (Matthew 11:28).

✧ Read the description of the craftsman in the "Eckhart's Words" section.
✦ Does this image appeal to you?
✦ What "pieces" are you cutting away to realize Christ's presence in your life?
✦ Which people in your life reveal the light of Christ to you?
✦ Light a candle, give thanks for Christ's intimate presence in your life, rest in the quiet, and let the candlelight fill your heart.

✧ Choose a passage from the Gospels that speaks to you personally. Write it down on a small piece of paper and carry it with you for a week. Remain open to ways that you can integrate the meaning of this passage into your life.

✧ Drawing on Luke 2:1–20, enter into the following meditation:

> Imagine yourself at the cave in Bethlehem where Christ was born. . . . What does the cave look like in the darkness? . . . Smell the hay, . . . the animals, . . . and the night air. Draw close to the cave and touch it. . . . You see Mary and Joseph hovering over the child. What expressions are on their faces? . . . Turn your attention to the child, and let your heart open to his presence. . . . When you are ready, walk over to the manger, lift up the child, hold him close, . . . and speak to him. . . . Now close your eyes and rest in Jesus' presence.

✧ Ponder this question: When did you first witness the birth of Christ's love in your life?

✧ Write a dialog with Jesus. Ask him questions about his life and his suffering. Let him know what is occurring in your life. At the end of your dialog, let go of your words and images and rest in the silence, trusting in Jesus' loving presence.

God's Word

"Come to me, all you that are weary and are carrying heavy burdens, and I will give you rest. Take my yoke upon you, and learn from me; for I am gentle and humble in heart, and you will find rest for your souls. For my yoke is easy, and my burden is light." (Matthew 11:28)

Whoever says, "I have come to know him," but does not obey his commandments, is a liar, and in such a person the truth does not exist; but whoever obeys his word, truly in this person the love of God has reached perfection. . . . Whoever says, "I abide in him," ought to walk just as he walked. (1 John 2:4–6)

Closing prayer: "May Jesus also come into us, throw out and get rid of all obstacles, making us one as he is one with the Father and the Holy Spirit—one God. That we so become one with him and remain so eternally, may God help us. Amen" (McGinn, ed., *Teacher and Preacher*, p. 243).

✧   **Meditation 5**   ✧

True Detachment

Theme: In order to experience union with God in the depths of the soul, we need an attitude of detachment.

Opening prayer: Let me learn true detachment, God of my heart. Draw me away from all that keeps me from you, and make my heart pure and simple, receptive to your presence.

About Eckhart

In Eckhart's time a widespread craving for poverty was beginning to appear. This was in reaction to the growing material wealth of western Europe, which was connected to the expansion of commerce that began in the thirteenth century. The economic disadvantages of the lower classes stood out in stark contrast to the new wealth of the merchant classes, a wealth that deeply affected the church as well as every part of society.

Eckhart's teaching on detachment and the ideal of poverty should be recognized as a religious response to the historical situation in which he found himself. He preached a practice of poverty that went beyond a life of begging, wandering, and preaching. It was spiritual poverty—detachment from the things of the world—and it entailed, in imitation of Christ, a life of material poverty as well.

In one of his sermons, Eckhart exhorted his listeners to detachment this way:

> Therefore, make a start with yourself, and abandon yourself. Truly, if you do not begin by getting away from yourself, wherever you run to, you will find obstacles and trouble. . . . People who seek peace in external things— be it in places or ways of life or people or activities or solitude or poverty or degradation—however great such a thing may be or whatever it may be, still it is all nothing and gives no peace. People who seek in that way are doing it all wrong; the further they wander, the less will they find what they are seeking. . . . Truly, if a man renounced a kingdom or the whole world but held on to himself, he would not have renounced anything. (Colledge and McGinn, trans., *Essential Sermons*, p. 249)

Pause: Uniting with God means stripping away the illusions that veil our true nature and God's. What is one critical illusion or lie in your life now that keeps you from union with God?

Eckhart's Words

> If I want to write on a wax tablet, it does not matter how fine the words may be that are written on the tablet, they still hinder me from writing on it. If I really want to write something, I must erase and eliminate everything that is already there; and the tablet is never so good for me to write on as when there is nothing on it at all. In the same way, if God is to write on my heart up in the highest place, everything that can be called this or that must come out of my heart, and in that way my heart will have won detachment. (Colledge and McGinn, trans., *Essential Sermons*, p. 292)

> Consider a simile of this: A door, opening and shutting on a hinge. I compare the planks on the outside of the door

with the outer man, but the hinge with the inner man. As the door opens and shuts, the outside planks move backwards and forwards, but the hinge remains immovable in one place, and the opening and shutting does not affect it. (*Essential Sermons*, p. 291)

And you must know that to be empty of all created things is to be full of God, and to be full of created things is to be empty of God. (*Essential Sermons*, p. 288)

Reflection

Eckhart begins with the truth that as human beings who have lost our orientation to God and have become entangled in sin, we need to recover our God-centeredness. This is difficult, he suggests, because often in our living, our mind and heart are crowded with distractions, and we have little awareness of the power hidden within. We should become empty vessels so that we can discover God's ground as our ground and can allow the influence of this discovery to permeate us.

In order to do this, according to Eckhart, we need to detach ourselves from preoccupations with the needs of self and become open to the ground of our life. Begin with the self, he says, because that is the root of all our difficulties. Like a true spiritual director, Eckhart does not let us overestimate our spiritual aptitude: "Take a look at yourself, and whenever you find yourself, deny yourself. That is the best of all" (Colledge and McGinn, trans., *Essential Sermons*, p. 250). He also reminds us that we need to enter the path of detachment not of our own accord but because the fire of love has drawn us aside and invited greater commitment. When we recognize that the transient, limited things of this world no longer hold us captive as they once did, then we slowly turn away from them to face the God who calls us and for whom our heart hungers.

What does Eckhart mean by detachment? It involves consciously setting aside thoughts and images that repeatedly demand our attention. With single-minded focus we need to lessen the clamor in our head and place ourselves, silent and attentive, before a loving God. The initial effort is difficult and will cause suffering, counsels Eckhart, but with practice and patience, the process of surrender becomes more natural and easy. The promise: "In return for my going out of myself for love of him, God will wholly become my own" (*Essential Sermons*, p. 282).

This active form of detachment is accompanied by a passive form: "this annihilation and diminution of the self, however great a work it may be, will remain uncompleted unless it is God who completes it in the self" (*Essential Sermons*, p. 280). For example, events themselves, setbacks and painful events such as serious illness, offer the opportunity to spend less time and energy concentrating on our desires and reinforcing our self-image. We may be called to accept unjust attacks on our self-image in a manner that allows us to retain an inner balance and to not forfeit our inner life. Using Eckhart's image, we swing back and forth like a door with the motion of changing life events, yet we remain on a stable hinge, anchored in place.

Even spiritual practices do not necessarily move toward union with God because a person could be acting from self-interest rather than according to God's will. More important than practice is the attitude of "letting go," of open receptivity to divine presence in the fluctuations of everyday life. According to Eckhart, the more free we are from our own likes and dislikes—our attachment to ways of thinking or to emotions—the more open we are to union with God at any time and in any place.

The detachment that Eckhart asks from us does not eliminate self-giving or compassion, but influences the way we serve others. Through detachment our service is less influenced by preconceptions and emotional agendas. We have more psychic space between ourselves and others because our own self-image is less obtrusive, and as a result, we act more effectively. We can truly let people be, that is, we can love them for who they are. The fruit of detachment is not a cold, removed personality but a warm, joyful person who extends unconditional love.

Finally, in detachment and humility, I let go of all that I have and even what I am in order to be at home in the uncreated center of my being—God's own creating act.

✧ List some of the major obstacles to spiritual growth in your life. Which one is God inviting you to attend to at this time? How have you responded to this invitation?

Now list signs of spiritual renewal in your life. Which one has called for most of your attention? How have you responded to these signs of growth?

Conclude this review with a prayer asking God for the strength to remain open to the seeds of divine revelation.

✧ Reread the second selection in the "Eckhart's Words" section.

◆ Take a blank piece of paper and write a description of what you have planned for your life in the next year or so.
◆ Take another blank piece of paper and write a description of what you sense God is asking from you in the next year or so.
◆ Rest with these two points of view.
◆ Respond with an inner dialog with God.

✧ Take at least ten minutes to review the life events from the last week. Consider Eckhart's image of the swinging door that is anchored by hinges. Which events pulled you away from your inner sense of self? In which events did you retain an inner balance?

✧ We live in a time marked by world poverty, consumerism, and environmental blight. Many believe that we as human beings find our happiness through purchasing power. Eckhart offers a different understanding of human nature: only through detachment can we be fulfilled as human beings.

◆ Think of the consumer goods you depend upon. Consider whether your dependency covers up the source of life within. Open your life to God, and acknowledge the material images that prevent you from experiencing divine life.
◆ Assume a relaxed position and sit in stillness. . . . Experience the presence of a loving God, . . . and let go of thoughts and images that vie for your attention. . . . Let the Source of life heal you and answer the questions of your searching heart.

✦ Finally, cup your hands and raise them to God. Repeat a one-sentence prayer that seems appropriate to you, for example, "Jesus, fill my heart with love."

✧ Since true letting go lifts the heart, we need to celebrate the joy we receive from detachment. Sing or dance the life you have received from letting go!

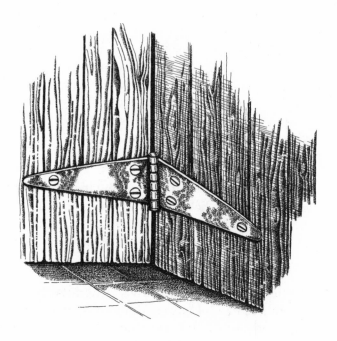

God's Word

I have been crucified with Christ; and it is no longer I who live, but it is Christ who lives in me. And the life I now live in the flesh I live by faith in the Son of God, who loved me and gave himself for me. (Galatians 2:19–20)

Closing prayer: "My soul is like a house, small for you to enter, but I beg you to enlarge it. It is in ruins; I ask you to rebuild it" (Sée, ed., *St. Augustine*, p. 68).

✧ **Meditation 6** ✧

Letting Go of "God"

Theme: The way of detachment calls us to leave behind not only ideas of the self but ideas of God as well.

Opening prayer: O God, your ways are beyond my comprehension; let me worship you in your mystery and not rest content with my present ideas of you.

About Eckhart

Though the following excerpt is considered apocryphal, it could well reflect the departing words the Meister shared with his disciples before embarking on a journey:

Meister Eckhart was [asked] by his good friends, "Give us something to remember, since you are going to leave us." . . .

[He said,] "Some people want to find God as He shines before them, or as He tastes to them. They find the light and the taste, but they do not find God. A scripture declares that God shines in the darkness, where we sometimes least recognize Him. Where God shines least for us is often where He shines the most. Therefore we should accept God equally in all ways and in all things. (Walshe, trans. and ed., *Sermons and Treatises*, vol. 3, pp. 147–148)

Pause: Ask yourself, Have I ever found God in the darkness?

Eckhart's Words

I say that whoever perceives something in God and attaches thereby some name to him, that is not God. God is above names and above nature. . . . Yet those names are permitted to us by which the saints have called him and which God so consecrated with divine light and poured into all their hearts. And through these we should first learn how we ought to pray to God. (Colledge and McGinn, trans., *Essential Sermons,* p. 204)

When God forms himself and pours himself into the soul, if you perceive him as a light or as being or goodness, if you know the least little bit of him, that is not God. You must realize that one has to pass over the "little bit" and must remove all additions and know God [as he is] one. (McGinn, ed., *Teacher and Preacher,* p. 322)

In good truth, [the spirit] is as little satisfied with God as with a stone or a tree. It never rests, it bursts into the ground from which goodness and truth come forth and perceives it [God's being] *in principio,* in the beginning, . . . before it acquires any name, before it bursts forth. (*Teacher and Preacher,* p. 315)

Reflection

According to Eckhart, detachment means not only letting go of ideas about ourselves but also ideas about God. He preaches a God that is not to be identified with any of the finite, limited things of creation, but a God who cannot be grasped by the senses, adequately imagined, or totally understood. If we chatter about God, he says, we are telling lies, because we cannot say anything or understand anything about God.

As a result Eckhart wants us to abandon our conceptions and preconceptions about God. Richard Woods comments, "Even our images of God must be stripped away, for all such images, in so far as they are our images, do not present God but only *our* concepts of God or those of the culture around us" (*Eckhart's Way*, p. 118). This perspective leads Eckhart to announce: "You should so seek [God] that you find him nowhere" (Colledge and McGinn, trans., *Essential Sermons*, p. 192).

· No doubt images of God have value, especially at the beginning of our relationship with God when, in emotional fervor, we attribute to God human qualities like kindness, patience, and wisdom. These images stoke the embers of the heart and eventually cause it to flame. However, Eckhart counsels that at the appropriate time in our development, we may be called to withdraw these projections and go directly to God. Ultimately we hunger for union, for a relationship that reaches beyond images.

Eckhart uses startling language in his sermons to make his point: "So therefore let us pray to God that we may be free of 'God'" (*Essential Sermons*, p. 200). Through these dramatic words, he tries to jerk us out of our habitual ways of thinking about God. Perhaps Eckhart's voice catches the attention of those today who may be uncomfortable with the image of God found currently in books and workshops that blend popular psychology and theology devoted to fulfilling self-potential. Forgotten is the incomprehensible God who draws us beyond ourselves and reminds us of our smallness in the face of mystery.

When a young person rejects God upon reaching adulthood, this person is primarily rejecting the incomplete childhood notion of God inherited from authority figures, parents, and the church, understood in a pre-adult way. In fact this rejection often does not signal loss of faith but authentic spiritual growth. Our concept of God should continually change throughout our life and lead us to an awareness of God as mystery. God, declares Eckhart along with other apophatic mystics, is called "darkness," not to denote the absence of light but to point toward the presence of something brighter than our eyes have the capacity to receive.

Eckhart advises us to revere the images of God as "Father," "Son," and "Spirit," but not to rest in these images or consider them final. He encourages us to remain open to the time when images and ideas fall away and our yearning for God takes flight. In letting go of "God," we "let God be God" (*Essential Sermons,* p. 184). Ultimately we can unite with God only in darkness and silence, in what Eckhart calls the "silent desert." So we must learn to be at home in the darkness.

On a practical and spiritual level, if we are drawn to a union with an effable God, we cannot be satisfied with "searching for" God. Actively seeking God implies that we know what we are seeking. And, if this is the case, we will never find it. So we should be content to be lost, and we will be found without knowing it. Our hope is not in our attempts to reach God but in a humble awareness of our limitations.

How should we respond to a God who is incomprehensible, a silent desert? Eckhart tells us to sink into the hidden ground of our being, that secret space where divine and human merge, and simply wait in darkness with naked trust and hope for God's coming. When the soul dares to become empty, it makes room for God to enter and find rest.

✦ Recall your earliest image of God. What were you taught about God as a child? Do you remember the stories that surrounded your childhood images? How did your relationship with God change as a young adult? As a mature adult? What life experiences have influenced the way you perceive God? How do you relate to God now?

✦ Draw or create a design that represents your present relationship with God.

✦ Write a dialog with God. Let God speak to you about the possibility of a deepening relationship.

✦ How does this line from a poem by William Butler Yeats relate to your own experience of God: "Hatred of God may bring the soul to God" (*The Collected Poems of W. B. Yeats,* "Supernatural Songs, V"; p. 284)?

✧ In the classic tale *The Little Prince,* by Antoine de Saint Exupéry, a pilot crashes his plane in the Sahara desert and encounters a mysterious little boy. The boy coaxes the pilot to stop repairing his plane, let go of his fear of dying, and search for an unknown well in the desert. After periods of hesitation, the pilot finally follows the little boy and learns to trust him. Also, the pilot realizes that on some hidden level, he has been seeking a home for his heart ever since childhood. With the help of the little prince, he discovers that the desert, when it is entered with innocent faith, will indeed produce the abundant water of life.

✦ How does this journey into the unknown, into the silent desert, describe your own spiritual passage?
✦ How have you been led into the desert and asked to depend on naked faith?
✦ What happened to your image of God during this journey?
✦ What wisdom did you gain?

God's Word

Upon my bed at night
    I sought him whom my soul loves;
I sought him, but found him not.
(Song of Solomon 3:1)

[Jesus said,] "Do not let your hearts be troubled. Believe in God, believe also in me. In my Father's house there are many dwelling places. If it were not so, would I have told you that I go to prepare a place for you? And if I go and prepare a place for you, I will come again and will take you to myself, so that where I am, there you may be also." (John 14:1–3)

Closing prayer:

One thing have I asked of you, Yahweh,
this I seek:
to dwell in your house
all the days of my life,
to behold your beauty
and to contemplate on your Temple.

. . . .

Wait for Yahweh;
be strong, and let your heart take courage.
Yes, wait for God!

(Psalm 27:4,14)

✧ **Meditation 7** ✧

Freedom

Theme: By letting go of thoughts and images of both the self and God, we become free to respond to an infinite love.

Opening prayer: God of truth, give me the grace to attain the freedom that you want for me.

About Eckhart

The inner freedom that Eckhart espoused, a life of the spirit that was removed from achieving status, success, and all the complexities these would bring, contrasted sharply with other church leaders of the time who sought power and prestige. The papacy and the ecclesiastical hierarchy were known for their corruption, decadence, and greed. The Avignon papacy, which existed from 1309 onward, came to stand in all its sumptuous splendor as a sign of the degradation of spiritual values. It is no surprise that reformers such as Catherine of Siena raised their voices against ecclesiastical decadence.

In a Europe devoid of respect for ecclesiastical leaders, people were open to new religious ideas and revolutionary movements unaffiliated with the church structure. Others took their search inward. The Beguines and Beghards, the Friends of God, and many Dominican nuns and monks increasingly found solace in a personal relationship with God—in mysticism.

It is significant that the Meister's description of inner freedom in his sermons to lay people appealed to his listeners. But it also would have been perceived as threatening to church leaders striving to suppress heresies of various kinds, to control unofficial groups of spiritual seekers, and to preserve collapsing ecclesiastical and institutional structures.

Pause: Ask yourself, When have I realized that I do not possess an inner freedom? Bring to mind the circumstances that surrounded this awareness.

Eckhart's Words

Now pay great attention and give heed! I have often said, . . . that a man should be so free of all things and of all works, both interior and exterior, that he might become a place only for God, in which God could work. (Colledge and McGinn, trans., *Essential Sermons*, p. 202)

The person who has abandoned all things where they are lowest and transitory receives them again in God where they are truth. All that is dead here is life there, and everything that is coarse and material here is there spirit in God. It is just as if someone poured pure water into a clean barrel that was completely spotless and clean and let it become still; and if then a person put his face over it, he would see it on the bottom just exactly as it is as part of himself. This happens because the water is pure and clean and unmoving. This is how it is with all those people who exist in freedom and unity in themselves. (McGinn, ed., *Teacher and Preacher*, p. 289)

The person who does not regard himself or anything else but God alone and God's honor is truly free and rid of all mercantilism in all his works and seeks nothing of his own, just as God is free and unencumbered in all his works and seeks nothing of his own. (*Teacher and Preacher*, pp. 240–241)

Reflection

Eckhart insists that inner freedom can only be found through detachment. It is impossible, he says, to seek detachment without at the same time desiring freedom.

We sometimes think we are free and able to make the most suitable choices for ourselves, yet we do not realize that our freedom is dramatically restricted when it is not grounded in truth. As a result of this deception, our plans often go awry and we wander aimlessly looking for answers.

Our difficulty, the Meister suggests, stems from our irrational attachment to things, people, circumstances, the spiritual path, or our image of God. All these restrict freedom because the soul becomes preoccupied with whatever it is pursuing and ignores the inner dimensions of life. Attachments also control the soul through emotional entanglements. When we inordinately care for something, it possesses the power to lift us to the heights of joy or drop us into the depths of despair. A soul preoccupied by such attachments forfeits an inner sense of self and the possibility of emotional stability. It is distracted and, as a result, unable to experience the spontaneity and joy of inner freedom in a relationship. The work of "letting go" prepares the soul for absolute openness to the Word of God, where it can receive all things in truth: "Now a heart that has pure detachment is free of all created things, . . . and so it achieves the highest uniformity with God, and is most susceptible to the divine inflowing" (Colledge and McGinn, trans., *Essential Sermons,* p. 293).

According to Eckhart, inner freedom is possible because the innermost depth of the human soul is not subject to time and space or to any external influence. It is subject to God alone. God rests in the temple of the soul and calls it home. Eckhart encourages us to turn inward with seriousness and make room in our soul. We do not have to make anything happen—simply remain detached and let the inner light guide us.

When we are actually free, our choices reflect not self-will but God's will. Thus we discover a sense of openheartedness toward all and a freedom that cannot be disturbed, no matter the suffering or loss. Even if we wander away from God, Eckhart assures us, the moment we turn back "all lost time is restored" and we recover our true state of freedom (*Essential Sermons*, p. 184).

✧ Read the following poem:

The emptier I do become,
the more delivered from the Me,
the better I shall understand
God's liberty.

(Franck, trans., *The Book of Angelus Silesius*, p. 130)

✦ Make a list of the primary restrictions on your inner freedom: for example, physical or emotional wounds, anger, jealously, greed, an inability to trust in the love of God and the love of others.

✦ When you are finished, pray to the Spirit of Jesus for guidance and support in your journey toward greater freedom.

✧ The road to freedom is strewn with fallen idols: the false god, the false self, the false image of God's creatures. Ask the Spirit of Jesus to reveal the truth in your life. Throughout the day repeat a short prayer that rises from your need to be free, for example, "Christ Jesus, set me free."

✧ What image occurs to you when you answer the question, "What is God's will in my life?" Is it a force pressing down on you from the outside? Is it a fountain springing up from within?

✦ Imagine God's will as a personal presence dwelling at your center and activating your power to choose.

✦ Now reread the "Eckhart's Words" section.

✦ How has your perspective toward doing God's will changed or deepened?

✧ Ponder Eckhart's image of a person looking into a clean barrel of water and seeing her true face (see the "Eckhart's Words" section). Consider the following questions:

✦ Do you believe that the innermost ground of your soul is free from time and space and even from personality?

✦ If the water of your inner life was still and you could see your true face, what would it look like?

✦ Take some time for quiet, and reflect on the inner life that lies deep below the surface of ordinary, everyday existence.

✧ Bring to mind the lack of freedom in the world: oppression through war and violence, false political ideologies, social injustices. Respond to this lack of freedom with a symbol of truth. Find an appropriate symbol, or create it: fly a kite, paint, dance, enjoy the laughter of a friend.

God's Word

Now the Lord is the Spirit, and where the Spirit of the Lord is, there is freedom. And all of us, with unveiled faces, seeing the glory of the Lord as though reflected in a mirror, are being transformed into the same image from one degree of glory to another; for this comes from the Lord, the Spirit. (2 Corinthians 3:17–18)

Closing prayer: Awaken me, liberating God, to the freedom I already have but do not realize. Release me from the conditions that keep me enslaved and unable to act authentically for myself and for others.

✧ Meditation 8 ✧

Pray Always and Everywhere

Theme: The spiritual life does not consist of finding a particular way of praying or favorite spiritual exercises. Rather, the spiritual life encompasses the entire life of a person.

Opening prayer: Teach me, divine Companion, to be attentive to you not only when I frequent the sacraments and worship but in every facet of my life.

About Eckhart

In one of his sermons, Eckhart relates the following story:

> Someone once asked a virtuous person why it was that he sometimes had an urge for devotion and prayer and at other times he had no urge at all. He replied thus: "The hound that catches sight of a hare, catches its scent, and comes upon its tracks, and so chases the hare. Then the others see this one giving chase, and they take up the chase, too. But they quickly tire and give up. So it is with a man who has caught sight of God and has caught his scent. He does not give up but keeps up the chase. . . . Such a man does not tire; but others tire quickly." (McGinn, ed., *Teacher and Preacher,* pp. 309–310)

Eckhart recognized the difference between one who has "caught the scent" of the object of pursuit and those who pursue motivated by the action of other pursuers.

Eckhart, in another sermon, compares prayer to a thirst and a quenching of thirst:

> It is like a [person] consumed with a real and burning thirst who may well not drink and may turn his mind to other things. But whatever he may do, in whatever company he may be, whatever he may be intending or thinking of or working at, still the idea of drinking does not leave him, so long as he is thirsty. The more his thirst grows, the more the idea of drinking grows and intrudes and possesses him and will not leave him. (Colledge and McGinn, trans., *Essential Sermons*, p. 253)

Pause: Ponder these questions: Do I limit my prayer to certain times and practices? Does it ever emerge as an undercurrent in my daily life?

Eckhart's Words

Praying is a better work than spinning, and the church is a better place than the street. But you ought in your works to have a like disposition and a like confidence and a like love for your God and a like seriousness. Believe me, if you were constant in this way, no one could come between you and the God who is present to you. (Colledge and McGinn, trans., *Essential Sermons*, p. 252)

We ought to pray so powerfully that we should like to put our every member and strength, our two eyes and ears, mouth, heart and all our senses to work; and we should not give up until we find that we wish to be one with him who is present to us and whom we entreat, namely God. (*Essential Sermons*, p. 249)

A [person] cannot learn this by running away, by shunning things and shutting himself up in an external solitude; but he must practice a solitude of the spirit, wherever or with whomever he is. He must learn to break through things and to grasp . . . God in them. (*Essential Sermons*, p. 253)

Reflection

Eckhart teaches that detachment leads to a particular way of prayer that opens us to the deepest center of our being and allows us to live out of that center: "Yes, one Hail Mary said when a man has abandoned himself is more profitable than to read the Psalms a thousand times over without that" (Colledge and McGinn, trans., *Essential Sermons*, p. 260).

The prayer that Eckhart describes involves leaving behind ideas of self and God. We need to consciously set aside thoughts and images that crowd the mind and distract it from its true focus—the divine Presence. If the flow of consciousness can be imagined as a river, then on the surface we find the floating debris of thoughts and emotional energy that feed our self-image. On the deepest level, we find a still center. Eckhart invites us to dive deep where we can remain naked and attentive before God.

People usually think of forms of prayer. It was common in Eckhart's era to concentrate on set formulas for prayer: reciting the psalms, the Pater Noster, the Ave Maria, or reading from prayer books that were collections of prayers. Eckhart, however, was not interested in this or that method but in an attitude. Authentic prayer involves a radical transformation of attitude that pervades all aspects of daily living from writing a letter to attending a liturgy. It means living in a way that allows us to let go of attachments and respond to God.

Eckhart recognized that particular times set aside for prayer are critical, especially because they are reservoirs of spiritual energy that help us cope with the chaos of an active life, but he emphasizes the need for prayer in the midst of the everyday work and play. Praying must become a thirst that pervades all aspects of our consciousness, a growing desire to find God in all places and at all times.

A story is told about two Zen monks, both avid smokers. Each of them consulted their spiritual advisers about smoking during prayer time. One was chastised by his adviser, the other received praise and reinforcement. The monk who had been admonished asked his friend who was praised what he had told his adviser. "I asked," the monk replied, "whether it was permissible to pray while smoking." The Meister, like the adviser, would have approved of this monk's question.

Eckhart suggests that prayer in its highest form is not asking for favors but asking for communion with God. If prayer means wanting something from God or asking God to take something away, then a detached heart seeks to be "free of all prayer" (*Essential Sermons*, p. 292). Eckhart is not suggesting that we dismiss prayers of petition or ignore the needs of others in our prayers, but he insists that the perfection of prayer is not in saying prayers but in simply remaining open to God's presence. Through our detachment our prayers encompass more than we can imagine. According to Richard Woods, Eckhart is advocating "the highest form of prayer, one in which the welfare of the entire world is not only included but advanced because of the universal solidarity of humankind in God through Christ" (*Eckhart's Way*, p. 121).

Personal preferences for certain prayer techniques or times of solitude often become comfortable. They are ways of temporarily releasing tension and recharging the spirit so that we can return to daily living. Yet these practices do not necessarily transform our life or lead to a conversion of heart. Old spiritual attachments retain their hold and continue to demand our attention, preventing true inner growth. Eckhart recognizes that prayer and solitude are necessary for spiritual growth, but he does not want them to block our surrender to God. He suggests praying always and practicing a solitude of spirit wherever we go.

✧ Reread the first two selections of the "Eckhart's Words" section, and reflect on your own way of praying. How do you respond to Eckhart's call to an increasing thirst for God in all that we do? Write or draw a prayer that reflects your deepest desire for God.

✧ Go for a walk or catch up on some work. During the activity continue to remain aware of God's presence. It is not necessary to focus on God but rather allow God's presence to "color," or add a dimension, to your activity. As you become more involved in the activity, rest deeper in the divine Presence.

✧ One prayer that seems appropriate to Eckhart's way is centering prayer. This prayer involves letting go of thoughts and images and waiting upon God with loving attentiveness. To practice centering prayer, follow these steps:

✦ Choose a sacred word as a symbol of your intention to remain open to the mystery of God's presence beyond images and thoughts.

✦ Assume a comfortable position and close your eyes; gently introduce the word as a way of acknowledging God's presence within.

✦ Whenever thoughts or distractions occur, gently return to the sacred word.

✦ At the end of a fifteen-minute period, sit in silence for a few minutes and then slowly recite the Our Father.

(If you have questions about this form of prayer, consult these resources: *Open Mind, Open Heart,* by Thomas Keating; and *Centering Prayer,* by Basil Pennington.)

✧ Eckhart says that solitude is not primarily a place but a solitude of spirit, a total commitment that we take with us everywhere. Out of this solitude, we share God's life in us with others. One way of practicing this solitude is to let people be themselves even though they may unsettle or aggravate you. When you feel that you are forgetting your solitude because you are distracted by someone's personality, simply calm down, recall your solitude, and return to a genuine compassion for others. Practice this solitude for a day or so, and see what happens.

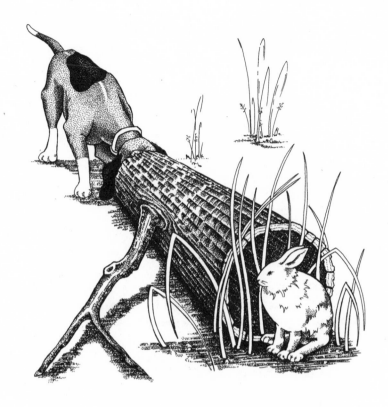

God's Word

"Be dressed for action and have your lamps lit; be like those who are waiting for their master to return from the wedding banquet, so that they may open the door for him as soon as he comes and knocks. Blessed are those slaves whom the master finds alert when he comes. . . . If he comes during the middle of the night, or near dawn, and finds them so, blessed are those slaves." (Luke 12:35–38)

Closing prayer: Loving God, I reach out for you, yearn for you who remains hidden in darkness. Let my longing become my prayer; let it enkindle a spark in the depths of my soul.

A Still Silence

Theme: Silence leads us into the depths of God where the Word is spoken in the Trinity, and into our own depths where the same utterance is born in the believing soul.

Opening prayer: Ineffable God, let silence lead me into the depths of my being, to the core where I can discover what is real and true.

About Eckhart

As a Dominican, Eckhart not only taught and preached but nourished a contemplative spirit. He practiced meditation and silent contemplative prayer. Dominic emphasized the need for silence, in part for effectiveness in teaching and preaching, and in part to counterbalance a friar's active life in the busy environment of medieval towns.

One of Eckhart's key themes is silence: not only the silence of the environment or the silence before and after conversation but the mystic silence at the center of the soul. In one sermon we find a typical piece of advice, "Your spirit should be elevated, not downcast, but rather ardent, and yet in a detached, quiet stillness" (Walshe, trans. and ed., *Sermons and Treatises*, vol. 1, p. 36).

Yet this is a silence that needs to be practiced. Perhaps, like us, Eckhart availed himself of the opportunities that were part and parcel of the flow of an ordinary day: in the silence that fills a child's face when he or she smiles; the silence in the gaze of two lovers; the silence that encompasses an elderly couple walking hand in hand; the silence that radiates from a worker's hands; the silence of a night sky; the silence of deer running, hawks soaring, birds flitting; the silence of snow falling, trees blossoming, boughs swaying; the silence that surrounds an old pair of shoes or a loved one's shirt.

Entering into this silence, "letting things be" in quiet attention, disposes us to the silence at the center of the soul.

Pause: Ask yourself: Do the words that I speak have a connection with the silence at the center of my being? Do I tend, in the spirit of our times, to cover over this silence with noise and chatter?

Eckhart's Words

Sometimes I have spoken of a light that is uncreated and not capable of creation and that is in the soul. . . .

. . . In the innermost part, where no one dwells, there is contentment for that light, and there it is more inward than it can be to itself, for this ground is a simple silence. (Colledge and McGinn, trans., *Essential Sermons*, p. 198)

If someone else but Jesus alone speaks in the temple (that is, the soul), then Jesus keeps silent as though he were not at home. And he is not at home in the soul then because it has other guests with whom it is conversing. But if Jesus is to speak in the soul, it must be alone and must itself remain silent if it is to hear Jesus speak. Yes, then he enters in and begins to speak. What does the Lord Jesus say? He says what he is. And what is he? He is the Word of the Father. (McGinn, ed., *Teacher and Preacher*, p. 242)

The very best and noblest attainment in this life is to be silent and let God work and speak within. When the powers [i.e., of thought, imagination, and sensation] have been completely withdrawn from all their works and images, *then* the Word is spoken. (Walshe, trans. and ed., *Sermons and Treatises*, vol. 1, pp. 6–7)

Reflection

Eckhart tells us that we are unable to hear the Word spoken in the depths of our being because we have ignored it and have not cultivated the silence necessary to hear: "The Word lies hidden in the soul, unnoticed and unheard unless room is made for it in the ground of hearing, otherwise it is not heard; but all voices and all sounds must cease and perfect stillness must reign there, a still silence" (Walshe, trans. and ed., *Sermons and Treatises*, vol. 1, p. 257).

If we could only have space to hear, we would be awestruck. Silence allows God to awaken our consciousness and nurture it, drawing us toward a secret exchange of love: "That is the kiss of the soul, . . . there the Father bears his Son into the soul, and there the soul is spoken to" (Colledge and McGinn, trans., *Essential Sermons*, p. 205).

Prayer heightens our awareness of certain images that repeatedly distract us: anger, worries about money or job, jealousy, health issues—whatever pushes its way into our consciousness with energy. We need to take these before God, hand them over, perhaps again and again, and trust in God's healing power. As a result the pool of silence deepens and becomes more real.

The power of silence cuts the deep roots of attachments that lie beyond our knowledge and our effort. Thomas Keating writes, "The deeper your interior silence, the more profoundly God will work in you without your knowing it" (*Open Mind, Open Heart*, p. 83). At times we find ourselves resting in this silence, in the same way that two people who love each other feel no need to talk and who simply remain present to each other. This silence feeds a relationship, makes it stronger, and provides room for even greater communication. Words that rise from this silence enrich the relationship rather than hide it. Truthful words spoken frequently lead to a deeper silent communion.

Eckhart tells us that we should learn to think and act in such a way that the interior silence can be preserved. At first we need to recognize the importance of silence and to cultivate it through detachment. Eventually we will discover an inner solitude that can be retained wherever we may be. This sense of solitude implies that the silence is no longer passive but dynamic, something with energy that stays with us and guides us throughout the day.

The more we are in touch with silence, the more we find the voice of God resonating through our life in all that we hear. We trust God beyond images and understanding, God who is known as simple presence in the darkness. Through grace a profound work takes place in the silence—the hidden ground of our soul will be united with God's hidden ground: "Be silent and at rest so that the soul can rest in God" (McGinn, ed., *Teacher and Preacher*, p. 173).

✧ Practice silence during your time for prayer by letting go of all thoughts and images as gently as morning dew falls from a blade of grass. Resisting thoughts is itself a thought, because you invest emotional energy in the process and become more frustrated when your efforts fail. Don't let yourself become annoyed at the number of distractions, but simply and gently, with the help of a word or phrase that expresses your intent, return to God's presence. In pure faith you know that God is communicating within you even though nothing appears to be happening.

✧ Read a favorite passage from the Scriptures, reflect on the passage for a time, say a prayer that rises up in your heart, and then take time to remain silent in God's presence.

✧ When your mind becomes unsettled during the day, take time to follow your breathing. Do this not simply as a relaxing exercise but as a way of centering in God's presence.

✧ Practice remaining open to the flow of silence that greets you throughout the day.

✦ List some of the silences you have encountered that are similar to those mentioned in the preceding "About Eckhart" section.

✦ Read over the list slowly, and let these silences resonate with the silence within you.

✦ If you feel the need, express in writing, drawing, dance, or song whatever is rising out of the silence in your heart.

✧ Jesus wants to be alone in the silent temple of our heart, says Eckhart. This calls for a daily practice of detachment. Practice letting go of your personal preferences throughout the day. When the opportunity presents itself, choose to relinquish your own desire and to be open to other options. For example, rather than continuing with your own plans and goals, you may find yourself in a position to help a person by listening to them or by driving them to a destination.

✧ When we practice releasing control of our life, Eckhart reminds us that our intention should not be to impose undue hardship on ourselves but to increase our response to the gentle guidance of God's love. With this intention at work as we let go of control, we create room in our heart for greater silence. Jesus has room to be at home within us.

God's Word

. . . While gentle silence enveloped all things,
and night in its swift course was now half gone,
your all-powerful word leaped from heaven, from the
royal throne.

(Wisdom 18:14–15)

Closing prayer: "For God alone my soul waits in silence; / from [God] comes my salvation" (Psalm 62:1, NRSV).

Birth of the Word in the Soul

Theme: The Incarnation did not occur only when God became human in Bethlehem two thousand years ago; it also occurs continually in the most secret and inward part of ourselves, the ground of the soul.

Opening prayer: Silent Source of life, may your Word come to birth in me.

About Eckhart

Scholars have suggested that, even though Eckhart is not the kind of mystic who likes to describe visions, he seems to be relating an autobiographical experience in one of his sermons. He describes the following dream vision:

> It appeared to a man as in a dream—it was a waking dream—that he became pregnant with Nothing like a woman with child, and in that Nothing God was born, He was the fruit of nothing. God was born in the Nothing. (Walshe, ed., *Sermons and Treatises*, vol. 1, pp. 157–158)

Pause: Ponder this: Do I consider Jesus Christ to be mostly an external, historical figure, or do I also find him somehow present at the center of my daily life?

Eckhart's Words

And as it has already been said about emptiness or nakedness, as the soul becomes more pure and bare and poor, and possesses less of created things, and is emptier of all things that are not God, it receives God more purely, and is more totally in him, and it truly becomes one with God, and it looks into God and God into it, face to face, as it were two images transformed into one. (Colledge and McGinn, trans., *Essential Sermons*, p. 222)

That is what the text means with which I began: "God has sent his Only-Begotten Son into the world." You must not by this understand the external world in which the Son ate and drank with us, but understand it to apply to the inner world. As truly as the Father in his simple nature gives his Son birth naturally, so truly does he give him birth in the most inward part of the spirit, and that is the inner world. Here God's ground is my ground, and my ground is God's ground. (*Essential Sermons*, p. 183)

And I have often said that there is a power in the soul that touches neither time nor flesh. It flows from the spirit and . . . is wholly spiritual. In this power God is always verdant and blossoming in all the joy and the honor that he is in himself. That is a joy so heartfelt, a joy so incomprehensible and great that no one can tell it all. For it is in this power that the eternal Father ceaselessly brings his eternal Son so to birth. (*Essential Sermons*, p. 179)

Reflection

The letting go of self as well as the letting go of our understanding of God, both through our own efforts and through

God's grace, prepare the heart in its depths for the birth of the Word.

For Eckhart, the meaning of the Incarnation is not limited to historical events recorded in the Scriptures, but it is an act taking place now in the depths of the soul. He does not deny that Jesus was a historical figure, but prefers to envision him as transcending space and time as the Word of God. Neither are we primarily historical, the Meister asserts, because our ultimate fulfillment cannot be found in history but only in God.

The question is, God may have become human, but do we believe that God also entered the most inward and secret part of our being beyond space and time? If we answer "Yes," then Eckhart assures us that Christ resides at the center of each of our lives and will do so for all time and for eternity.

According to Eckhart, God, vibrant with life, pours out into the Trinity, overflows into creation, giving birth and bearing the Word in us. The image Eckhart offers us is one of God who lies in childbed like a woman and gives birth in every receptive soul. This image has parallels in the Bible, in Isaiah 42:14, where God is described as "cry[ing] out like a woman in labor"; and in Isaiah 66:9, where God brings the fruit of the womb to a quick delivery. Referring to those who participate in this process, the Meister calls them "mothers who take great joy in the child born within" (adapted from McGinn, ed., *Teacher and Preacher*, p. 330).

How is God being born in a person? When a person uncovers the divine image within that was created at birth, then the image of God becomes visible. Through the Fall we have lost our innocent relationship with the birth of the Word, Eckhart tells us, and we have become attached to things that have clouded our vision. But by releasing ourselves from attachments, we awaken to an inner light that we recognize as having been present all along.

"Giving birth is to be [understood] here as God's revealing self" (*Teacher and Preacher*, p. 301). Eckhart cautions us not to anticipate the birth as a personal experience—some vision, ecstasy, or deep state of consciousness. Richard Woods explains, "It is, moreover, not an experience so much as it is a sudden and yet progressive realization of presence, a union with God rooted in eternity, obscured by time, space and matter, but susceptible of being rendered conscious even in this life" (*Eckhart's Way*, pp. 124–125). The more open we are to God's presence, the more we recognize that the birth is constantly occurring in the soul.

Now that we are no longer pulled in every direction and we realize the birth of God's Son in us, we experience both joy and rest. "Throw out all sadness from your heart so that nothing but constant joy is in your heart," Eckhart advises (*Teacher and Preacher*, p. 330). Joy is ours, he tells us, and can never be taken away, because through the birth of the Word, we share in God's own peace and joy.

Finally, through the birth of God in the soul, our vision expands: "All things become simply God to you, for in all things you notice only God, just as a man who stares long at the sun sees the sun in whatever he afterwards looks at" (Walshe, trans. and ed., *Sermons and Treatises*, vol. 1, p. 45).

Even though this birth involves an inner journey, it engages us in the world in a way that allows us to see God's presence everywhere and to help in a way that is truly compassionate. We discover the Incarnation at the heart of physical reality, and we participate in its work.

✧ Choose a piece of music that represents birth for you. Listen to the music, and let it fill you with promise and hope.

✧ Describe, in writing, the times when you felt Christ's presence born in your life: through the Scriptures, in the liturgy, through friends and family, through nature.
+ Read your description aloud to yourself, or share it with a friend.
+ Read Romans 8:35–39.
+ Offer a prayer of praise to God.

✧ Write a dialog with Christ. Ask him questions about his presence within you. Let him lead you to your deepest ground. Finish your dialog by resting in Christ's presence.

✧ Make a list of the signs of hope and joy in your life.
+ Include the names of the people who give you a sense of peace.

✦ Read the list and the names slowly, and with each one offer a short prayer of thanksgiving.
✦ Light a candle, and read the section entitled "God's Word."

✧ Review the ways in which you have extended Christ to others in the past few days. Thank the Spirit of Christ for working through you. Sing a hymn of thanksgiving.

God's Word

When a woman is in labor, she has pain, because her hour has come. But when her child is born, she no longer remembers the anguish because of the joy of having brought a human being into the world. So you have pain now; but I will see you again, and your hearts will rejoice, and no one will take your joy from you. (John 16:21–22)

Closing prayer: Word of God, I pray for the grace of your birth in the depths of my life. May I become who and what I was created to be; may I receive the gift of divine life according to your will.

✧ Meditation 11 ✧

Contemplation in Action

Theme: "But whoever really and truly has God, . . . has [God] everywhere, in the street and in company with everyone, just as much as in church or in solitary places or in [one's own] cell" (Colledge and McGinn, trans., *Essential Sermons*, p. 251).

Opening prayer: God of infinite love, let me be awake and attentive to your call in my daily life. Give me the strength to respond to my relationship with you as I go about my daily activities.

About Eckhart

The fourteenth century was an era of mystical fervor. While mystics such as Catherine of Siena, Julian of Norwich, Henry Suso, Jan van Ruysbroeck, and others, experienced and wrote about the heights of mystical prayer, there was another development—lay piety. Lay people, due to increased literacy and local preaching, had access to mystical teaching and were encouraged to envision their life in the context of the spiritual quest. Meister Eckhart reinforced this connection between the Christian life of the laity and the lives of great mystics by preaching the Scriptures and the foundations of faith. Using the language of mysticism, he emphasized that the ordinary active life, when carried out with awareness of God's presence, was the highest ideal.

The Meister himself knew what it meant to practice contemplation in the busyness of daily activity. He was not a hermit but an active and responsible man. He spent his days counseling, preaching, and supervising a number of religious houses.

In carrying out his responsibilities, Eckhart traveled long distances on foot between the houses. In this era of cities and trading, the roads were sometimes thoroughfares traveled by multitudes of people; at other times the roads were desolate and overrun with robbers. By example and by word, Eckhart maintained that the spiritual life need not be a quiet life. Rather, it was more ordinarily an active life of service in which one maintained a simple union with God. He practiced what he preached:

> People ought to learn to be free of their works as they perform them. For a man who has not practiced this, it is hard, learning to attain to a state in which the people around him and the works he performs are no hindrance—and much zeal is needed to achieve this—so that God is present to him and his light shines in him undiminished, whatever the occasion, whatever the environment. (Colledge and McGinn, trans., *Essential Sermons*, p. 274)

Eckhart explores the relationship between the contemplative and the active life through the story of Mary and Martha, found in Luke's Gospel. The story typically identifies Mary with the higher contemplative life because she remained at the feet of Jesus, focusing only on him; and Martha with the active life because she busily prepared for her guest. Eckhart, with his unique interpretation, reverses the emphasis.

He prefers Martha's way because she is able to remain anchored in God's presence while serving her neighbor. In both ways she draws close to God. Her activity retains a contemplative dimension. Because she is free and detached, she prays through her work.

Pause: Consider these issues: Are there times when I use prayer and the spiritual life as a way to avoid service to others?

Are there times when I use service to others to avoid a conscious relationship to God?

Eckhart's Words

Now Martha says, "Lord, tell her to help me." This was said not in anger, but it was rather affection that constrained her. We can call it affection or teasing. How so? Observe. She saw how Mary was possessed with a longing for her soul's satisfaction. Martha knew Mary better than Mary knew Martha, for she had lived long and well, and life gives the finest understanding. (P. 80)

Therefore Christ spoke as if to say: "Never fear, Martha, she [Mary] has chosen the best part: this will pass. The best thing that can befall a creature shall be hers: she shall be blessed like you."

. . . Martha was so well grounded in her essence that her activity was no hindrance to her: work and activity she turned to her eternal profit. (Walshe, trans. and ed., *Sermons and Treatises*, vol. 1, pp. 86–87)

Reflection

When God's presence comes alive for us through the birth of the Word, we naturally want to extend the love and joy we experience. We carry it within us as we turn to the world and to others with a deeper sense of responsibility. The hope and creativity we find in the divine birth in us drives us toward a deeper and freer engagement in community life and social change.

Eckhart's vision could be described as one in which God creates the world and then, through those who discover hope and creative energy of God's presence within them, draws the world back toward God. We become cocreators with God. We share God's compassion and activity. Because detachment has made room for the birth of the Word, God can work through us freely to shape the earth. Deepening union with God bears fruit in our activities and has important consequences for our vocation.

Eckhart makes the point that God can be found everywhere and especially in every activity. We should not become attached to special places or specific approaches to divine presence. In our day, for example, we should not be tempted to imagine that extended time in a hermitage is necessary for us to truly engage in contemplation or that those in contemplative orders have the best opportunity for union with God.

People who are married and supporting a family can, in their commitments and detachments, let life teach them and let God be present to them. God's ways are not limited by our lifestyle and responsibilities. Eckhart warns, "When people think that they are acquiring more of God in inwardness, in devotion, in sweetness and in various approaches than they do by the fireside or in the stable, you are acting just as if you took God and muffled his head up in a cloak and pushed him under a bench" (Colledge and McGinn, trans., *Essential Sermons*, p. 183).

In another comment, Eckhart makes it clear that he recognizes that praying is better than hauling stones and that a church is a better atmosphere than the market, but he insists that a particular activity or place is not as important as the spirit, the inner attention, we bring to it: "It is not what we do that makes us holy, but we ought to make holy what we do" (*Essential Sermons*, p. 250).

✧ Like Martha, all Christians are invited to remain inwardly detached and anchored in God's presence. Use the following passage from Matthew's Gospel to reflect on your life at this stage:

"You shall love the Lord your God with all your heart, and with all your soul, and with all your mind." This is the greatest and first commandment. And a second is like it: "You shall love your neighbor as yourself." (Matthew 22:37–39)

✧ Eckhart always accents—perhaps to a fault—the inner life: "God has no regard for what your works are, but for what your love and devotion and intention in the works are" (*Essential Sermons*, p. 265).

✦ Reflect on three major activities of an ordinary day.
✦ Ask yourself: What kind of dedicated energy do I bring to these activities? What am I intending to do as I go about them?

✧ Reread the Mary and Martha story in the "Eckhart's Words" section.
✦ Following Eckhart's interpretation, whom do you identify with, Mary or Martha?
✦ Do you believe that a contemplative dimension, the sense of remaining anchored in God's presence, can be retained in a busy life?
✦ How do you balance the active and the contemplative life? The outer and inner activities? Can you do this without stress? Can you find ways to improve the balance?
✦ Dialog with Eckhart, as with a spiritual director, about your own desire to be a contemplative in your action.

✧ Identify and list the needs of some persons who are significant in your life.
✦ Which of these needs calls for your participation in some way?
✦ Make specific plans to respond to one of these needs or to one of these persons.
✦ Pray to Christ for wisdom and strength to help this person and, at the same time, to continue to harbor your inner life.
✦ Write a prayer for this, and use it periodically as you set out to address these needs.

✧ Choose a brief prayer that would center you during an activity. Go for a long walk, and integrate the prayer with the rhythm of your breathing. Walk slowly, be present to the moment, and enjoy your surroundings. You might use, "We ought to make holy what we do."

✧ Eckhart tells us that the birth of the Word within our soul pours out into expressions of love.
✦ Take time to recall the events of this day.
✦ Bring to mind the acts of love you extended to others.

- ✦ On what occasions could you have shown a greater capacity to love?
- ✦ Can you foresee any way that you can extend love to others tomorrow?
- ✦ Offer a prayer of thanksgiving for the Spirit's work in you.

God's Word

Now as they went on their way, [Jesus] entered a certain village, where a woman named Martha welcomed him into her home. She had a sister named Mary, who sat at the Lord's feet and listened to what he was saying. But Martha was distracted by her many tasks; so she came to him and asked, "Lord, do you not care that my sister has left me to do all the work by myself? Tell her then to help me." But the Lord answered her, "Martha, Martha, you are worried and distracted by many things; there is need of only one thing. Mary has chosen the better part, which will not be taken away from her." (Luke 10:38–42)

Closing prayer: Let me learn to live, O God, in touch with the ground of my soul so that all my activity will be connected to it.

✧ **Meditation 12** ✧

In the Service
of God's Word

Theme: The abundant life of God within us overflows into service to God's Word according to our unique talents.

Opening prayer: Creator God, give me the words, gestures, and actions to express the truth you have placed in my heart.

About Eckhart

Eckhart lived during a time of hopelessness and despair. A worldview that had depended on a balance of power between church and state, a sense of economic and religious stability, and shared language and values was beginning to fade. With little sense of hope in the temporal future, a fascination with end time and eternal destiny prevailed.

The gap between rich and poor was widening. In 1315, peasants suffered famine due to floods and torrential rains. The rural population shifted to the towns and cities, and with an increase in number came a decrease in the availability of food and shelter. Migration to towns resulted in overcrowding and unemployment. The poor became poorer, and the rich became richer.

The collapse of older ecclesiastical and institutional structures created a vacuum of meaning. People searched for a new order to replace the old. As a result, mysticism became a viable alternative because it provided a resource for belief and a meaning for life in this world and for eternal happiness with God.

In this atmosphere of hopelessness and suffering, Eckhart preached to groups of lay people and religious men and women. He offered his listeners a perspective on inner stability and freedom at a time when the old securities were disintegrating and fears were raging. The dynamism of his message and the creative language that he employed appealed to his listeners and was, in turn, informed by their concerns.

Eckhart's sermons were not private reflections but an extension of his role as spiritual guide to religious and laity alike. His sermons may have been profoundly serious, but they also possessed a buoyancy, a lightheartedness, that was accented by verbal playfulness. This is not surprising for the words of a preacher who seems to have experienced the joy of the mystic, which is Christ's birth in his own soul. However, Eckhart's poetic disposition was not appreciated by the interrogators of the Inquisition: "It was the poetry they could not appreciate, the daring excesses of speech and flights of imagination by which the great scholar transcended the arid limitations of the learned disquisition and dispute, seeking to move his listeners by the art of preaching" (Woods, *Eckhart's Way*, p. 215).

Those who listened no doubt found some of Eckhart's points difficult to understand, but at the same time they recognized that they were spoken by one who had touched, and been touched by, the Source of truth in his own life. Eckhart himself was so compelled to share his message that he once declared that if people came to hear him he was happy, but even if no one were to come, "I would still have had to preach it [the sermon] to the collection box" (Frank Tobin, *Meister Eckhart: Thought and Language*, p. 183).

Pause: Ponder these questions: Have I an opportunity to share my faith commitment? In what way do I best do this?

Eckhart's Words

As I was coming here today I was wondering how I should preach to you so that it would make sense and you would understand it. Then I thought of a comparison: If you could understand that, you would understand my meaning and the basis of all my thinking in everything I have ever preached. The comparison concerns my eyes and a piece of wood. . . . If it happens that my eye is in itself one and simple (Mt. 6:22), and it is opened and casts its glance upon the piece of wood, the eye and the wood remain what they are, and yet in the act of vision they become as one, so that we can truly say that my eye is the wood and the wood is my eye. But if the wood were immaterial, purely spiritual as is the sight of my eye, then one could truly say that in the act of vision the wood and my eye subsisted in one being. If this is true of physical objects, it is far truer of spiritual objects. (Colledge and McGinn, trans., *Essential Sermons*, p. 197)

I once said whatever can be expressed properly in words must come forth from within and must have movement from an inner form; it cannot enter in from without but must come out from within. It lives actually in the innermost [part] of the soul. There all things are present to you, are living within and seeking, and are in their best and highest [state]. Why do you not notice any of this? Because you are not at home there. (McGinn, ed., *Teacher and Preacher*, p. 249)

The Father spoke a Word; this was his Son. In this single Word he spoke all things. Why did he only speak one Word? Because all things are present to it [the Word]. If I could encompass in one thought all the thoughts I ever had or ever shall have, I would have but a single word; for the mouth utters what is in the heart. (*Teacher and Preacher*, p. 335)

Reflection

In the tradition of Dominic and his followers, who called themselves the Order of Preachers, Eckhart's primary concern was preaching. In the spirit of this tradition, Eckhart immersed himself in silence, meditation, and contemplation as a preparation and foundation for good and effective preaching. This spirituality was grounded in the Word and in service to the Word. Eckhart's sermons were deeply rooted in biblical themes. Each of them was based on a scriptural text which was expanded by a multitude of scriptural references, a method commonly used in medieval times. As a believer, Eckhart approached the text with reverence and wonder. As a preacher, he uncovered layers of the text in a search for deeper meaning, surprising and amazing the listener with the treasures he would bring to the surface.

Eckhart makes it clear that when we are at home in ourselves, our speech and actions reflect the one Word that we bear in our heart. The dynamism of this Word flows and overflows: our lives become like musical instruments played by a divine Artist, and our resulting song praises God and influences the hearts of others.

Service to God's Word does not have to be limited to preaching from a pulpit but may take different forms in a variety of contexts: speaking softly or waiting silently at the bedside of a dying person; listening to the lonely and comforting them with appropriate gestures; defending publicly the integrity of those who suffer the loss of dignity; taking time to assist the elderly or instruct the young; writing fair-practice policies in the workplace.

Whenever we extend the Word to others through speech and action, we become like the prophets. We stand for the truth that we have uncovered in our heart that urges us to speech. Truth will find its resonance in the heart of others, stirring them to response.

✧ We serve God's Word in many ways: a mother passes along wisdom to a daughter, a father to a son; we model spiritual lives to others in and through our regular words and actions; and we serve others' needs responsibly in daily living.

✦ Who are the individuals who express God's word to you through their life?

✦ Who do you influence through your own modeling of the Christian life?

✦ Complete this sentence: For me, serving God's word has taken the form of . . .

✧ If a young women or young man asked you for advice on the inner life (bring to mind someone in particular), what would you share with them? Write your answer in letter form.

✧ Is there anything about your spirituality that you would like to share with a spouse or a friend? Determine that you will do so when the opportunity presents itself.

✦ Share your faith journey with an individual or group that is open to your message.

✦ When have you felt the need to speak out on an issue that was rooted in Christian values? How did you respond?

✧ How have you given witness to Gospel values today?

✦ Share the message of the Gospel with a child. Because children learn primarily through activity, you might pray together, find quiet time together, share a meal, listen. When a child asks you why you make certain choices, you have the opportunity to talk about your spiritual values.

✧ Reread the "Eckhart's Words" section, reflecting on the oneness of the wood and the eye in the act of vision. Spend at least an hour in the following exercise of the senses (seeing, hearing, smelling, touching, tasting). Do this to understand what Eckhart means by "oneness" in act.

✦ Find one object to use for each sense.

✦ Become aware of yourself as you see, hear, smell, touch, or taste the object.

✦ Become attentive to the object as you see, hear, smell, touch, or taste it.

✦ Become alert to the oneness in act as you engage with each object.

✦ Take your time in doing and completing this exercise. Before you close, reread Eckhart's words.

✦ During the day, try to be at one in your actions.

God's Word

In the presence of God and of Christ Jesus . . . I solemnly urge you: proclaim the message; be persistent whether the time is favorable or unfavorable; convince, rebuke, and encourage, with the utmost patience in teaching. . . . Always be sober, endure suffering, do the work of an evangelist, carry out your ministry fully. (2 Timothy 4:1–5)

Closing prayer: God, give me strength to cooperate with your divine activity in the world, to proclaim your word from the depths of my being. Give me the courage I need in the face of disapproval, the gratitude I need in the face of approval.

✧ **Meditation 13** ✧

In Suffering, Hold Fast to God

Theme: Because creation is finite and wounded, human life in this world involves suffering. God's presence can make suffering transformative.

Opening prayer: Merciful God, companion in my trials, I pray for the courage to face suffering, so that through it, I can find union with you.

About Eckhart

Before and during his trial, Eckhart seems to have ignored the threat of being tried and executed. The prosecutors attacked the content of his teaching as well as the misleading effect of his words on the laity. Eckhart either conceded or rejected minor points, but upheld the correctness and orthodoxy of his teachings as a whole. He died while awaiting the results of his appeal to the pope. Though we cannot know what he was thinking or feeling during this process of the inquisition or how he would have reacted to the condemnation of some of his propositions that came after his death, we can assume that he embraced the counsel that he passed along to others:

Whether it be sickness or poverty, hunger or thirst, or whatever it might be—whatever God has ordained or not ordained for you, or whatever God gives you or does not give you, all this is the best for you. Be it that you have no sense of spiritual devotion or the interior life, or whatever you have or do not have, if you really direct yourself toward intending God's honor in all things, then whatever he does with you is the best. (McGinn, ed., *Teacher and Preacher*, p. 248)

Pause: What forms of suffering—illness, setback, diminution of self, loss of relationship—have you experienced recently?

Eckhart's Words

If you want to be free of all affliction and suffering, hold fast to God, and turn wholly to him, and to no one else. Indeed, all your suffering comes from this, that you do not turn in God and to God and no one else. (Colledge and McGinn, trans., *Essential Sermons*, p. 211)

In this power [of the soul] God is ceaselessly gleaming and burning with all his riches, with all his sweetness and with all his joy. Truly, there is such delight and such great, immeasurable joy in this power that no one can tell or reveal it all. But I say: If there were a single man who were to contemplate rationally and truly in this for an instant the joy and the delight that is there, everything that he could have suffered and that God would have wished him to suffer would be for him too little and, indeed, nothing; and I say more—it would always be his joy and his ease. (*Essential Sermons*, p. 180)

For truly, if anyone had denied himself and had wholly forsaken himself, nothing could be for him a cross or sorrow or suffering; it would all be a delight to him, a happiness, a joy to his heart, and he would truly be coming to God and following him. For just as nothing can grieve or afflict God, so nothing can make such a man rueful or sad. And, therefore, when our Lord says: "If any man will come to me, he should deny himself and take up his cross and follow me," it is not merely a command, as people usually say and think. It is a promise and a divine teaching about how all a man's suffering, all his work, all his life can become joyful and happy for him, and it is more a reward than a command. For such a man has everything he wants, and he wants nothing that is wrong; and that is blessedness." (*Essential Sermons*, p. 230)

Reflection

Eckhart wrote with profound insight on the subject of suffering, especially in the *Book of Divine Consolation* and the *Counsels of Discernment*. In these he refers to the necessary role of the cross in the life of the Christian. He does not dwell on suffering as an end in itself but demonstrates that it is a fact of life. His concern is to guide us through dark times.

If we try to escape this reality and attempt to lose ourselves in physical comfort and security, we will find no lasting peace, because these are incomplete, transitory, and unable to satisfy us. Anything we cling to inordinately will eventually become a source of suffering. In the Meister's words: "I run after created things, from which by their nature desolation comes, and I run away from God, from whom all consolation flows. Is it then surprising that I suffer and that I am sad?" (Colledge and McGinn, trans., *Essential Sermons*, p. 213).

Eckhart addresses spiritual suffering as well. The process of letting go of our attachments causes its own form of suffering. Unlike the suffering that comes from clinging to material goods, the suffering that comes from detachment, though painful, makes us stronger, wiser, and more at peace. We continue along the path of detachment because we experience an amazing freedom that nourishes our heart and pulls us toward our ultimate fulfillment.

At times suffering overwhelms us with its sheer horror. Eckhart counsels that instead of concentrating on the misery of suffering, we should focus our attention on God's love and the promise of everlasting joy. Commenting on the passage, "'If any want to become my followers, let them deny themselves and take up their cross and follow me'" (Matthew 16:24), he reassures us that we have been promised that all our suffering will be transformed. In other words, through suffering we can awaken to the possibility of true freedom in God, and this fills the heart with joy.

Moreover, he consoles those who suffer by reassuring them that God does not abandon us but remains in us and suffers with us: "God suffers with man, he truly does; he suffers in his own fashion, sooner and far more than the man suffers who suffers for love of him" (*Essential Sermons*, p. 233). Divine compassion transforms human misery.

✧ Eckhart highlighted the paradox in suffering when he wrote, "The greater the suffering in God's will, the more happiness there is" (McGinn, ed., *Teacher and Preacher*, p. 309). Have you experienced moments of great happiness in the midst of a difficult task? A searing love? A rejected effort? Reflect on one experience of this paradox in your life. Write a prayer of wonder and awe.

✧ Listen to music that draws you inward. Recall some of the losses you have experienced. Then choose a symbol of hope and beauty: a bouquet of flowers, a plant, a picture of a time in your life when you were happy, a gift from a spouse or friend. Place the symbol near you and, recalling God's nearness and love as well as the promise of transformation, repeat the following sentence several times: "Anyone who would come to me should forsake the self and take up the cross" (adapted from Matthew 16:24).

✧ Recall a time of suffering that was exceptionally difficult for you. What did the suffering teach you? What has changed in your attitude toward suffering since that time?

✧ Relax and place yourself gently in the presence of God.
✦ Believe that you are cherished and embraced by love.
✦ Read the following passage meditatively: "You have heard of the endurance of Job, and you have seen the purpose of

the Lord, how the Lord is compassionate and merciful"
(James 5:11).

✦ Ponder the depths of Christ's love for you, in the presence
of a crucifix.

✦ Conclude by following your breathing for five minutes.

✧ Retrieve the part of you that does not want to suffer,
that does not want to be aware of the suffering of others. Address it, and ask it to reveal itself. What is this part of you like?
How does it feel? Describe the part to yourself. It may be helpful to write your response. If you feel inclined, create a dialog
between the part of you that is open to suffering and the part
of the self that fears it.

✧ Read the following passage slowly:

My God, my God, why have you deserted me?
Far from my prayer, from the words I cry?
I call all day, my God, but you never answer;
all night long I call and cannot rest.
Yet, Holy One,
you who make your home in the praises of Israel—
in you our ancestors put their trust;
they trusted and you rescued them.

(Psalm 22:1–4)

✦ Listen to Jesus' voice, the agony and loneliness.

✦ Listen, also, to the cries of the poor, the suffering, the distressed—all the lonely and persecuted people of every time
and every culture.

✦ Listen to your own voice, the agony of your own cry.

✧ It is rare to meet someone who suffers without complaint and with calm, joyful acceptance.

✦ Recall a person, young or old, who impressed you first with
their tranquillity and about whom you later learned of some
chronic suffering.

✦ Bring to your awareness your own desire to turn to God
fully. Ask God for the help you need to gain strength and
perspective on your suffering.

✦ Pray for the gift of trust and tranquillity beyond the suffering.

God's Word

Sing for joy, O heavens, and exult, O earth;
    break forth, O mountains, into singing!
For the LORD has comforted his people,
    and will have compassion on his suffering ones.
.   .   .   .
Can a woman forget her nursing child,
    or show no compassion for the child of her womb?
Even these may forget,
    yet I will not forget you.

(Isaiah 49:13–15)

Closing prayer: Merciful God, companion in my trials, you promise that suffering can become joy for me. Give me the strength to suffer for your sake and to deny all that leads me away from you. May I experience the happiness of someone who truly desires to come to you.

✧ Meditation 14 ✧

The Just Will Live

Theme: The just person knows that life, and the powers of life, come not from one's self but from God.

Opening prayer: Keep me mindful, O God, that you are the source of my life. From you I come, to you I go.

About Eckhart

Eckhart must have caught the attention of listeners when he offered this description of the just person:

> They live eternally "with God," directly close to God, not beneath or above. They perform all their works with God, and God with them. Saint John says: "The Word was with God" (Jn. 1:1). It was wholly equal, and it was close beside, not beneath there or above there, but just equal. When God made man, he made woman from man's side, so that she might be equal to him. He did not make her out of man's head or his feet, so that she would be neither woman nor man for him, but so that she might be equal. So should the just soul be equal with God and close beside God, equal beside him, not beneath or above.
>
> Who are they who are thus equal? Those who are equal to nothing, they alone are equal to God. The divine being is equal to nothing, and in it there is neither image

104

nor form. (Colledge and McGinn, trans., *Essential Sermons*, p. 187)

Eckhart was not only dedicated to his fellow Dominican friars, he appeared to have a deep appreciation of the nuns and the Beguines who lived in the neighboring area. He dedicated himself to the spiritual guidance of these women and demonstrated an appreciation of women's intellectual and spiritual equality with men. This sense of equality may not have originated in the social or political milieu but in the belief that God is the creator and source of life, engendering each person's deepest identity. Each person comes from God and goes back to God. Through time and for eternity, each person becomes conformed to God.

Pause: How often throughout the day do you acknowledge that your life comes from God and offer a prayer of thanksgiving?

Eckhart's Words

"The just will live." Among all things there is nothing so dear or so desirable as life. However wretched or hard his life may be, a man still wants to live. . . . Why do you eat? Why do you sleep? So that you live. Why do you want riches or honors? That you know very well; but— why do you live? So as to live; and still you do not know why you live. Life is in itself so desirable that we desire it for its own sake. . . . Life is so precious that it flows without any medium from God into the soul. And because it flows from God without medium they want to live. What is life? God's being is my life. If my life is God's being, then God's existence must be my existence and God's is-ness is my is-ness, neither less nor more. (Colledge and McGinn, trans., *Essential Sermons*, pp. 186–187)

Now you might ask, "When is the will a just will?"
The will is complete and just when it is without any self-seeking, and when it has forsaken itself, and has been formed and shaped into God's will. . . . And in that will

you can accomplish everything, be it love or whatever you want. (*Essential Sermons*, p. 257)

The just man seeks nothing in his works. Those that seek something in their works or those who work because of a "why" are servants and hired hands. . . . You act just like a gardener who is supposed to plant a garden but only pulls out the trees and expects to get paid for it. This is how you ruin good works. (McGinn, ed., *Teacher and Preacher*, p. 296)

Reflection

The just person has a sense of human life flowing directly from God. This state represents the heights of Eckhart's spiritual path. Through the abandonment of will, the just soul attains a consciousness of its inner identity united with the divine ground. In Eckhart's words: "The just man is one with God. Like loves like. Love loves always what is like it. Hence God loves the just man like himself" (McGinn, ed., *Teacher and Preacher*, p. 265). As a result this person shares in God's attributes. The just person becomes justice; the good person becomes goodness.

Sharing in God's life, the just soul has a sense of emotional balance and remains at peace in the middle of affliction and conflict. The just person is also more able to freely choose what is right and good. The just soul has learned to live life as a power that flows directly from God. According to Eckhart, God rejoices—finds sheer delight—in the works of a just person.

Eckhart also describes the just person as one who, having become aware of the birth of the Word within, responds by "living without a why." Living without a why means doing whatever is appropriate without becoming personally captivated or attaching extrinsic motivations to one's actions. For example, when I worry about the results of my actions, I become distracted, and the activity becomes impaired. Living without a why means that attachment to results or to personal preferences no longer controls one's actions. A just person, then, with the help of grace, simply does what is intrinsically right.

God is the source of truly human actions, and the human soul's awareness of itself in God bears fruit in just actions. Eckhart says that this justice can be seen daily: "This way of being is so noble and yet so common that you do not have to spend a nickel or a penny on it. Just keep your intention proper and your will free, and you have it" (*Teacher and Preacher*, pp. 288–289).

Living without a why does not separate us from the world and our responsibilities. Just the opposite. Union with God overflows in our actions which, no longer hindered by willfulness, are more suited for the situation and the needs of others. The more we become will-less, the more we can let God's own goodness and justice flow through us and transform the world.

When Eckhart describes the state of a just person, he is not interested in attaching special experiences such as mystical ecstasy or rapture to it. He inspired his hearers not to look for the divine in unusual experiences but to search out the sacred in the everyday.

✧ Imagine that you are a tree flourishing at the side of a stream and that your life bears fruit in many good choices. Recall some of the good choices you have made in your life, choices that have come from the awareness of an inner truth. Ponder the wisdom in these choices, thank God for this wisdom, and close with the following passage: "It is no longer I who live, but it is Christ who lives in me. And the life I now live in the flesh I live by faith in the Son of God" (Galatians 2:20).

✧ What is the result of a life lived in the Spirit of Christ, the life of a just person? "The fruit of the Spirit is love, joy, peace, patience, kindness, generosity, faithfulness, gentleness, and self-control" (Galatians 5:22–23).

✦ Which of these signs do you see in your own life?

✦ Which of these signs is missing? Reflect on how this state of soul occurred.

✦ Choose one way that you can open yourself more to the guidance of the Spirit.

✧ When we perform actions without calculating their benefit to us, we live without a why. How does the following poem by Chuang Tzu apply to your life?

> When an archer is shooting for nothing
> He has all his skill.
> If he shoots for a brass buckle
> He is already nervous.
> If he shoots for a prize of gold
> He goes blind
> Or sees two targets—
> He is out of his mind!
>
> His skill has not changed. But the prize
> Divides him. He cares.
> He thinks more of winning
> Than of shooting—
> And the need to win
> Drains him of power.

> (Thomas Merton, "The Need to Win,"
> *The Way of Chuang Tzu*, p. 107)

✧ Those who live without a why discover freedom to be involved in society.
+ For whom and for what do you feel a sense of responsibility?
+ In what small ways have you served others today?
+ In what small ways have you served the planet?
+ Ponder your ability to help others without allowing your self- consciousness to get in the way.
+ Take a few minutes to follow your breathing, place yourself in God's presence, and read the following passage: "For you were called to freedom, brothers and sisters; only do not use your freedom as an opportunity for self-indulgence, but through love become [servants] to one another." (Galatians 5:13)

✧ Imagine that you are walking in a garden, the sunlight radiates everywhere, and you come to a rose. Allow the beauty of the rose to command all your attention; bend down and smell it. Now read the following poem:

She blooms because she blooms,
the rose . . .
Does not ask why,
nor does she preen herself
to catch my eye.
      (Franck, trans., *The Book of Angelus Silesius,* p. 66)

God's Word

Beloved, we are God's children now; what we will be has not yet been revealed. What we do know is this: when he is revealed, we will be like him, for we will see him as he is. And all who have this hope in him purify themselves, just as he is pure. (1 John 3:2–3)

Closing prayer: Let me remain open to your divine influence, my God. May your justice permeate my being. May my actions be linked to true contemplation, one will with yours.

✧ Meditation 15 ✧

Breaking Through

Theme: "Breaking through" is the culmination of the movement that began with the birth of the Word. It is a return to the Source of life and our true identity in God.

Opening prayer: Loving God, lead me into the desert silence where I find my heart's completion.

About Eckhart

As a good Dominican, Eckhart engaged in prayerful study. One of his favorite authors was Saint Augustine. Loosely following Augustine, Eckhart described six stages of the spiritual life that lead to mystical union.

In the first stage, the person follows the example of holy men and women in order to find spiritual balance. Then, the focus of one's attention turns more pointedly to the Scriptures and divine wisdom. In the third stage, the love and desire for God become the primary concerns and, like a beacon, guide the person through the dangerous waters of temptation and setbacks. In the fourth and fifth stages, the pilgrim becomes so deeply rooted in God's love that he or she is able to appreciate a deeper meaning in times of sorrow and to rest in an enduring inner peace. The final stage occurs when the person is no longer attached to this transient life and has been transformed into the divine image—in other words, has truly become God's child. This final stage, for Eckhart, involves both the birth of the Word in the soul and a mystical breaking through into the divine Godhead.

These stages easily flow into one another and should be understood as a gradual, steady awakening of personal discovery. As God's likeness is revealed more clearly, we hunger for oneness with the Source of all life. Eckhart writes: "Solomon says that all waters, that is all created things, flow and run back to their beginning (Qo. 1:7). That is why what I have said is necessarily true. Likeness and fiery love draw up the soul and lead it and bring it to the first source of the One" (Colledge and McGinn, trans., *Essential Sermons*, p. 221).

Some have suggested that Eckhart is alluding to his own breakthrough when he employs the first person in the following passages:

> This spirit must transcend number and break through multiplicity, and God will break through him: and just as He breaks through into me, so I break through in turn into Him. (Walshe, trans. and ed., *Sermons and Treatises*, vol. 1, p. 136)

> Here God's ground is my ground and my ground is God's ground. Here I live from my own as God lives from His own. (*Sermons and Treatises*, vol. 1, p. 117)

Pause: Consider the ways in which you find yourself drawn to the Source of all life.

Eckhart's Words

> I have spoken of a power in the soul which in its first outpouring does not take God as he is good and does not take him as he is truth. It seeks the ground [of God], continuing to search, and takes God in his oneness and in his solitary wilderness, in his vast wasteland, and in his own ground. Thus it remains satisfied with nothing else, but keeps on searching [to discover] just what it is that God is in his divinity and in the possession of his own nature. (McGinn, ed., *Teacher and Preacher*, p. 265)

It [the intellect] never rests, it bursts into the ground from which goodness and truth come forth and perceives it [God's being] *in principio*, in the beginning, where goodness and truth are going out, before it acquires any name, before it bursts forth. (*Teacher and Preacher*, p. 315)

In the breaking-through, when I come to be free of will of myself and of God's will and of all his works and of God himself, then I am above all created things, and I am neither God nor creature, but I am what I was and what I shall remain, now and eternally. (Colledge and McGinn, trans., *Essential Sermons*, p. 203)

Reflection

Whereas the birth of the Word in the soul begins the journey of the soul back to its deepest reality, breakthrough is the second and final stage of the journey leading to union. The detached soul is the locus in which both the birth of the Word and the breakthrough into the Godhead take place.

The soul, says Eckhart, will not rest until it finds complete union with the hidden ground behind the Trinity. As the divine image is revealed more clearly through growth in detachment, the soul hungers for the Source of all life: "Likeness and fiery love draw up the soul and lead it and bring it to the first source of the One" (Colledge and McGinn, trans., *Essential Sermons*, p. 221). In the end the trinitarian life to which a spiritual person is called is life in unity.

Eckhart stresses the oneness of the innermost ground of God. The mystical union that the soul discovers upon breaking through the divine ground is a union without distinction. In the Meister's era, God was considered to be "that greater than which cannot be conceived," a formula coming from Saint Anselm. Following this definition of God, creation is not and cannot be an addition to God. So Eckhart preaches: "No union is greater than that of God and the soul. When the soul receives a kiss from the divinity, it enjoys full perfection and happiness" (McGinn, ed., *Teacher and Preacher*, p. 265).

The Meister employs the metaphor of desert, or wilderness, to describe our ultimate identity with God. The desert is a trackless wilderness without name. However, the encounter with God in the desert is not sterile but rich and fruitful: "God leads this spirit into the desert and into the oneness of himself, where he is pure one welling up in himself" (*Teacher and Preacher*, p. 288). Though the wilderness may look forbidding to those who see it from afar, to the transformed heart, it represents the homeland. Just as the stark reality of the desert formed the Israelites into the People of God, the pilgrim soul, having been stripped through detachment, becomes fertile with God's life.

Breaking through, for Eckhart, does not remove the mystic from the world. All words and works are God's. The overflowing, creative energy of love binds the mystic to humanity and to the created order. Because of this sense of unity, the mystic no longer says "me" or "God" or "we." The darkness turns into light, a light in which the spiritual person becomes "one seeing," and shares this vision with the world. This is the reason that Eckhart can proclaim: "The eye in which I see God is the same eye in which God sees me. My eye and God's eye are one eye and one seeing, one knowing and one loving" (*Teacher and Preacher*, p. 270).

✧ Practice reclaiming your center in the following way:
✦ Sit comfortably in a quiet place.
✦ Close your eyes and turn inward, letting go of distractions, thoughts, and images.
✦ Become aware of the rhythm of your breathing. Feel your body relax, and find a center. Feel your mind grow more peaceful. Spend at least five minutes doing this.
✦ Experience the presence of Christ's love for at least ten minutes.

✧ Breaking through involves a journey into the Godhead, beyond all the usual names we use for God.
✦ Begin this practice by placing yourself in the presence of mystery.
✦ Believe that you are embraced and completely loved.
✦ Bring to mind a name that you prefer when addressing God. Repeat the name slowly and reverently, letting it form itself in your heart.

+ Be aware of all people and all creation gathering within you through the power of this name.
+ Let go of this name, and while remaining in the presence of mystery, sit into silence.
+ Remain in the fertile field of silence beyond all names and attend only to your breathing.

   ✧ Read Psalm 139 meditatively.

   Yahweh, you search me and know me.
   You know if I am standing or sitting.
   You perceive my thoughts from far away.
   Whether I walk or lie down, you are watching;
   you are familiar with all my ways.
   Before a word is even on my tongue, Yahweh,
   you know it completely.
   Close behind and close in front you hem me in,
   shielding me with your hand.

   . . . .

   Where could I go to escape your spirit?
   Where could I flee from your presence?

   (Psalm 139:1–7)

+ Ponder God's presence in your life during times of sickness and health, joy and sorrow, good fortune and bad. Then raise your heart in gratitude for God's abiding love.

   ✧ Eckhart uses the image of a desert to speak of the event of "breaking-through."
+ Find a handful of sand for this practice.
+ Relax for a few moments, . . . then feel the sand in your hands . . . look at it . . . bring to mind a desert landscape—hot during the day, cool at night, seemingly infinite waves of sand, hidden forms of life.
+ Think of the wildness of the desert: the unrestricted horizon, the sense of unlimited space, the rugged beauty, the stillness, the pure light. . . . This fierce land awakens silence in you; you are drawn beyond self-consciousness toward the rich mystery of life.
+ Now close your eyes and turn inward. Feel your heart's deepest desire—union with God beyond all restrictions, beyond distinctions or a sense of separateness.

✦ Is this sense of an unnameable desert part of your spiritual life? If so, remain present to it now, rest in it.

✦ Conclude by bringing your attention back to the sand in your palm. Recite the following verse three times:

> God will take great delight in you;
> God will quiet you with divine love.
>
> (Adapted from Zephaniah 3:17)

✧ With an awareness of the desert within, read these words of Eckhart's: "God leads this spirit into the desert and into the oneness of himself, where he is pure one welling up in himself" (*Teacher and Preacher,* p. 288). Ponder your own invitation to emptiness, to deeper silence, as an invitation to love more completely.

God's Word

Therefore, I will now allure her,
    and bring her into the wilderness,
    and speak tenderly to her.

(Hosea 2:14)

Closing prayer:

Alleluia!
We give thanks to you, Yahweh, for you are good.
Your love is everlasting!

. . . .

You led your people through the wilderness.
Your love is everlasting.

(Psalm 136:1,15)

O·N·E·N·E·S·S

✧ For Further Reading ✧

Colledge, Edmund, OSA, and Bernard McGinn, eds. *Meister Eckhart: The Essential Sermons, Commentaries, Treatises, and Defense.* New York: Paulist Press, 1981.

Forman, Robert K. C. *Meister Eckhart: Mystic and Theologian.* Rockport, MA: Element, 1991.

Fox, Matthew. *Breakthrough: Meister Eckhart's Spirituality in Transition.* Garden City, NY: Doubleday and Company, 1980.

McGinn, Bernard, ed. *Meister Eckhart and the Beguine Mystics.* New York: Continuum Publishing Company, 1994.

McGinn, Bernard, ed. *Meister Eckhart: Teacher and Preacher.* New York: Paulist Press, 1986.

Walshe, M. O'C. *Meister Eckhart: Sermons and Treatises,* volumes 1–3. Rockport, MA: Element, 1979.

Woods, Richard. *Eckhart's Way.* Wilmington, DE: Michael Glazier, 1986.

Titles in the Companions for the Journey Series

Praying with Anthony of Padua
Praying with Benedict
Praying with Catherine McAuley
Praying with Catherine of Siena
Praying with Clare of Assisi
Praying with Dominic
Praying with Dorothy Day
Praying with Elizabeth Seton
Praying with Francis of Assisi
Praying with Francis de Sales
Praying with Frédéric Ozanam
Praying with Hildegard of Bingen
Praying with Ignatius of Loyola
Praying with John Baptist de La Salle
Praying with John Cardinal Newman
Praying with John of the Cross
Praying with Julian of Norwich
Praying with Louise de Marillac
Praying with Meister Eckhart
Praying with Teresa of Ávila
Praying with Thérèse of Lisieux
Praying with Thomas Merton
Praying with Vincent de Paul

Order from your local religious bookstore or from

Saint Mary's Press
702 Terrace Heights
Winona MN 55987-1320
USA
1-800-533-8095